New
Directions in
American
Architecture

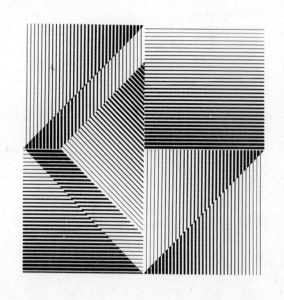

ROBERT A. M. STERN

NEW DIRECTIONS

IN

AMERICAN

ARCHITECTURE

GEORGE BRAZILLER   NEW YORK

Copyright © 1969 by George Braziller, Inc.

All rights reserved

For information address the publisher:

George Braziller, Inc.

One Park Avenue

New York, N.Y. 10016

Library of Congress Catalog Card No.: 70-81278

Jacket design by Toshihiro Katayama

Book design by Jennie Bush

Printed in U.S.A.

Third Printing, 1974

CONTENTS

PREFACE

This essay is not intended as a historical overview of the evolution of modern architecture in America, nor as a comprehensive analysis of the work of all the significant architects now practicing here. Rather, it is a partial presentation of designs by some of the most influential and innovative architects at this moment, whose work is viewed in relation to the development of their individual styles and to our most pressing urban problems. I have also sought to make clear the philosophical positions at the root of many current approaches to architecture and urban design.

In presenting the various points of view now being expressed, I have relied on quotation in order to make the book more immediate and to place as few barriers as possible between the reader and the architects and critics themselves. This will serve, in addition, to emphasize the intensity with which architects are thinking about their own work in relation to the issues of the day. I should like to caution the reader that my approach to the subject is that of a young member of the architectural profession and that the essay which follows must necessarily reflect my own involvement in the ongoing debate within the profession.

Barbara Leeds and my brother, Elliot M. Stern, were of invaluable assistance in the preparation of the manuscript; Craig W. Whitaker and Jonathan Stoumen provided useful assessments of direction of argument at an especially critical time. Thanks are due Martha Beall of the Braziller staff for securing the illustrations, always a burdensome task, and Janice Pargh, who was the best possible of editors— a patient and provocative critic.

January, 1969

INTRODUCTION

The influence of the third generation of modern architects is now making itself felt. The contribution of this new generation (and I use this term in reference to philosophical stance and not to age) must be seen in relation to the two which preceed it: the heroic generation of *form givers*, Le Corbusier, Mies van der Rohe, Frank Lloyd Wright, and the second generation of *formalists*, refiners and redefiners, Philip Johnson, Eero Saarinen, Paul Rudolph et al. among the Americans who, coming to maturity in the uncertain postwar years, sought stability through strong personal statement often removed from considerations of program and context.

The heroic generation of modern architects, coming to architectural maturity in the first third of this century, shared a belief in architecture as a primary force in culture; because architecture was to mold (even improve) life-styles, it tended to remove its references from the familiar surroundings of everyday life, seeking inspiration instead from outside cultures (Wright's obsession with Japan) and from the machine (Le Corbusier and Walter Gropius). Most of all, this brave new world was to replace all traces of earlier Western urban culture (especially that of the nineteenth century); Le Corbusier wished to tear down Paris (Voisin Plan, 1922–1925); Wright projected a continuous suburban sprawl across America (Broadacre City, 1930–1935) which would bring an end to the concentrated city as we still know it.

The second generation of modern architects seeks to adjust the forms of the first to a necessarily less abstract position (the economic depression of the thirties, the Second World War, and the current global and urban crises having relegated architecture to a less central role as a shaper of man's destiny). This effort to rethink the attitudes and the forms of the architecture of the twenties (the so-called International Style) has at last gone beyond the eclecticism of the early 1950's, the neohistoricism of Minoru Yamasaki, and the romanticism of Edward Durrell Stone, toward two positions: a rigorous, sculpturally active and obsessively complete one (coming out of Le Corbusier's and Wright's later projects and best seen in the work of Paul Rudolph) and an equally rigorous neoclassicism relying heavily on the example, if not always the forms, of Mies van der Rohe (best exemplified by the work of Kevin Roche and Philip Johnson).

The second generation of modern architects, now constituting the leadership of the profession, both in terms of public esteem and solid accomplishment, is pursuing goals quite opposite to those deemed appropriate by the third. The two philosophies that prevail have been described as "exclusive" and "inclusive" in intent.[1] The more established of the two, the exclusive approach, operating within the tradition of the orthodox modern architecture that has dominated advanced architecture since the 1920's (the late flowering of the International Style), seeks to construct a man-made world in accord with ideal formal and social images. It is the underlying philosophy of the second generation of modern architects. It deals in pure and simple shapes often at the expense of problem-solving. It is an attitude which separates problems of shape (universal and abstract in its view) from problems of function (particular and less significant). It is an attitude that is constantly searching for prototypical solutions for various programs (housing, civic centers, and so on). Its most complete architect is Paul Rudolph who, writing about the American work of Mies van der Rohe, upon which so much of this architecture depends, suggests the limitations and the strengths of this approach: "Mies makes wonderful buildings only because he ignores many aspects of a building. If he solved more problems his buildings would be far less potent."[2]

The inclusive point of view seeks a redefinition of architecture through the acceptance of what Robert Venturi, its most accomplished spokesman, describes as the "complexity and contradiction" of modern life. As a response to Mies's minimizing dictum, "less is more," Venturi says, "more is not less."[3] The inclusive approach rejects that heroic stance which orthodox modern architecture assumed to itself as the source of cultural values in favor of a more modest and flexible position in which architecture embodies the values which society, not just other architects, values and supports. It struggles to approach each problem on its own terms and rejects the prototypical solution in favor of the individual case.

A recent competition for an apartment house in the Brighton Beach section of Brooklyn illustrates the nature of this philosophical split in terms of architecture and urban design. The winning entry (*Fig. 1*) by Wells and Koetter seems more appropriate as a monumental grouping than as a housing scheme. Its composition of tower and low-rise housing, organized around a formal courtyard (and reminiscent of Mitchell/Giurgola's entry in the competition for the Boston City Hall; *see Figs.* 67–68), is strong but unrelated in design, vocabulary, and siting to the existing buildings in the neighborhood. It is instead intended as a prototypical solution for the generic problem—housing along the waterfront. The third-prize entry (*Fig. 2*), submitted by Venturi and Rauch, and having the consistent loyalty of three of the seven jurors, works within the vernacular of the adjacent speculatively built housing (bland brick boxes of the

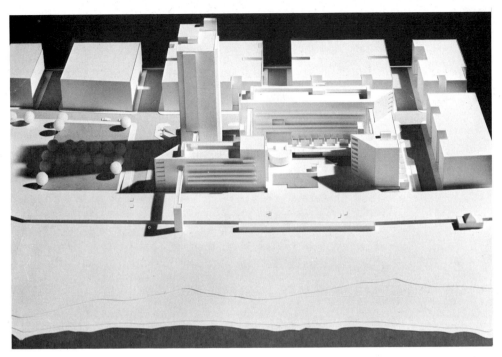

1. Jerry A. Wells and Fred Koetter: First-prize entry, competition for housing at Brighton Beach, Brooklyn, New York, 1968. Model.

2. Venturi and Rauch, Denise Scott Brown, Gerod Clark and Frank Kawasaki: Third-prize entry, competition for housing at Brighton Beach, Brooklyn, New York, 1968. Model.

1920's and 1930's. It is not monumental; it is not prototypical. "This split jury," according to Philip Johnson, its chairman, "is indicative of many problems in today's architecture and deserves full discussion and publicity. To the majority, of which I was one," Johnson writes, "the Venturi and Rauch entry seemed a plan of very ugly buildings. We [Johnson, José Luis Sert, Charles Abrams, and Samuel Ratensky] felt that the buildings looked like the most ordinary apartment construction built all over Queens and Brooklyn since the Depression, that the placing of buildings was ordinary and dull."[4]

To Donlyn Lyndon, one of the dissenting minority (Lyndon, Romaldo Giurgola, and Richard Ravitch), the entry "1) . . . has a modesty that is appropriate to the scale and location of the project. . . . The competition terms neither called for, nor allowed of major social or technological reform. . . . 2) The scheme does not detract from or demean the surrounding neighborhood. It respects, but is not bound by the existing order. 3) In our view it offers real benefits for the people who might occupy it rather than polemic satisfaction to those who consider it. 4) The method of building is intrinsically so simple that it could be built well, not meanly. We think this would contribute to the personal dignity of its occupants. 5) We think it in no way represents 'more of the same' but is instead a thoughtful use of existing possibilities. . . . 6) Our concerns do not in any way represent a triumph for practicality over 'beauty' but rather indicate a sincere effort to relate the criteria for judgment to the conditions of the problem. I am as uncomfortable with the word 'practicality' as I am with the word 'beauty'; each encourages over-simplification. . . . This scheme seems a well-ordered, carefully considered and appropriate response to the conditions of the problem. Nor is the form unrelated to the efforts of many of our contemporaries in the arts to find new relevance in forms to which the public has been accustomed."[5]

The irony of the split which the Brighton Beach Competition dramatizes extends deep into the philosophical basis of current practice. As Venturi puts it, "Architects are out of the habit of looking nonjudgmentally at the environment because orthodox modern architecture is progressive, if not revolutionary, utopian and puristic; it is dissatisfied with *existing* conditions. Modern architecture has been anything but permissive: architects have preferred to change the existing environment rather than enhance what is there. But to gain insight from the commonplace is nothing new: fine art often follows folk art. . . . we look backward at history and tradition to go forward; we can also look downward to go upward."[6]

The following essay will focus on this philosophical split, first by exploring the work of some representative practitioners, whose architecture typifies in its excellence the principles of the inclusive or exclusive point of view, and then by examining some of its implications for the design of cities.

THE ARCHITECTS

Louis I. Kahn

THE extent of the philosophic split now prevalent in American architectural theory can be measured in the work of leading practitioners of the second generation—Kevin Roche, Paul Rudolph, and Philip Johnson—and those of the third—Robert Venturi, Romaldo Giurgola, and Charles W. Moore. The transitional figure in this split, bridging the two generations, is Louis I. Kahn.

Kahn separates the making of buildings into a two-fold process leading from "Form" to "Design" and back again—thereby formulating a methodology that is the most workable and influential for architects at this time. "Design is a circumstantial act, how much money there is available, the site, the client, the extent of knowledge," Kahn writes, "Form has nothing to do with circumstantial conditions. In architecture it characterizes a harmony of spaces good for a certain activity of man." Thus, to talk about Form and Design is to talk about "realization, about the measurable aspects of our [architects'] work and about the limits of our work. . . ."[7]

Vincent Scully, the architecture critic, has written about Kahn's slow evolution as an architect with understanding and affection, so that there is no need to consider his work in depth here.[8] But even a brief survey of Kahn's architecture can be useful by bringing out the qualities which have made it, in the words of Romaldo Giurgola, "not only the indication of a method but also a warning which brings the architect closer to his principles."[9]

Even in Kahn's first major building, the Yale University Art Gallery, preceding his own articulation of "Form and Design," the abstract rigors of a Miesian vocabulary were made to respond to the circumstances of a unique site with multiple levels and diverse urban and suburban character and to a distinctly eclectic environment without lapsing into the spurious neohistoricism of the period (*Fig. 3*). His Richards Medical Research Building, probably the single most influential and imitated American building of the 1960's, combines individual tower groupings which are rigorous in their functional, spatial, and structural purity into a highly unorthodox and almost casual grouping that is both clustered and linear, using towers as street-defining buildings in a way that is probably unique in twentieth-century urbanism (*Fig. 4*). The toughness and the clarity of the imagery suggest a functionalism made monumental and grand, though, in fact, the buildings, not mindful enough of the demands for flexibility on the part of the scientists, do not work very well.

3. *Louis I. Kahn in association with Douglas Orr: Yale University Art Gallery, New Haven, Connecticut, 1951–53. View of north facade from Weir courtyard.*

4. *Richards Medical Research Building, University of Pennsylvania, Philadelphia, 1957–61. Exterior stair towers (right and left), laboratories (exposed), and four air-intake stacks from the south.*

Kahn is the first American architect of stature since the decline of the Beaux-Arts (the "public-library style" of the first quarter of this century) to look at the design of cities in an architectural way. His traffic scheme for central Philadelphia and his design-plan for the same area, as well as his greenway system, first proposed for the Mill Creek area in Philadelphia (and later used at Society Hill by I. M. Pei as well as in countless other cities), demonstrate a measure of concern that goes deep into the nature of city problems: *all* is considered, local and regional implications, commercial and civic development, the scale of man and motor (*Figs. 5–7*). Kahn's approach to the redesign of existing cities, different from so-called city planning, seeks to deal with land-use planning in three-dimensional terms establishing, on a scale appropriate to twentieth-century problems, those controls (streets, buildings, bulk, concourse levels, linked open spaces, and so on) necessary to inform the design of individual buildings so that the environment of a neighborhood can be defined

5. *Traffic scheme for central Philadelphia, project, 1951–52. Above, existing movement pattern; below, proposed movement pattern.*

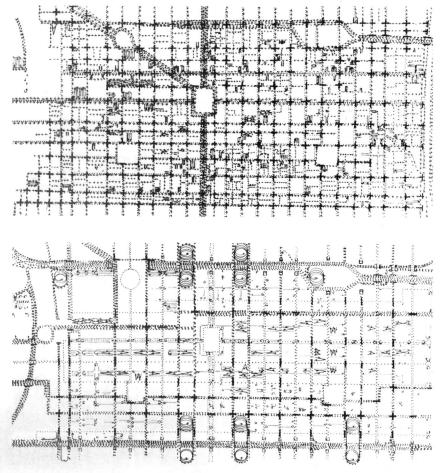

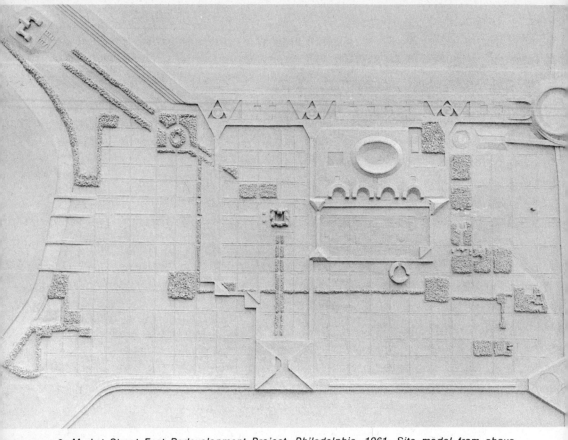

6. *Market Street East Redevelopment Project, Philadelphia, 1961. Site model from above.*

7. *Mill Creek Public Housing Project II, Philadelphia, 1959–62. Perspective drawing of site.*

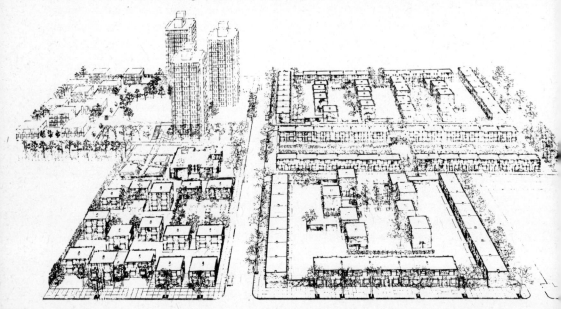

and made to reflect larger ideas and larger needs than that of individual building programs and individual building designs. "The City Planning profession," as David Crane (an architect and colleague of Kahn's at the University of Pennsylvania who has gone furthest in applying to actual projects Kahn's approach to city design) has pointed out, "is really an industry for dealing with urban problems, and within that industry there are many different professions that must become involved. And the architectural profession is one that must assume the role as the designer on a much bolder scale."[10] This approach of Kahn's, which has come to be described as concept planning, is concerned with hierarchy and location. The physical ordering of community values, it is, thus, a structural approach to city design rather than a graphic one.

Kahn's design for central Philadelphia, a project which he undertook in the early 1960's with the financial assistance of the Graham Foundation for Advanced Studies in the Fine Arts, is as much a comment on Philadelphia's own particular urban needs as it is on the needs of cities in general (*Fig. 6*). "The motor car has completely upset the form of the city," Kahn wrote in 1960, "I feel that the time has come to make the distinction between the viaduct architecture of the car and the architecture of man's activities. . . . The distinction between the two . . . could bring about a logic of growth and a sound positioning of enterprise."[11]

Kahn's center-city plan remains a form diagram; its translation into design is not likely. The highways are almost all there now, and in the places where Kahn proposed them, but the viaduct architecture is not with them; instead, there are the usual sewers of concrete, the realization of a design policy of slash and gash.

Kahn's design is nowhere more enigmatic than in his work at Dacca, in East Pakistan, where he is now building the Assembly Building (*Figs. 8–9*). It is impossible to predict at this time the ultimate success of this project. But its beauty of shape, the wonderful circles, triangles, and diamond cutouts, the utter power and utter simplicity in which all is composed, its obvious clarity and its obvious richness had already triggered a whole new loosening up of architectural composition even while it remained for some years a project, little more than a Form, in Kahn's terms. It is, nonetheless, a clear statement of Kahn's method, an illustration of his dependence on the particulate composition of Beaux-Arts design (separate pieces of space as opposed to design in orthodox modern architecture which depends on spatial flow) and his ability to adjust and inflect the rigid shapes of a geometry growing from that tradition to the immediate needs of a highly complicated program.

At Ahmedabad, India, in his work for the Indian Institute of Management, Kahn has realized his first major group of buildings at the scale of town planning (*Fig. 10*). A strong geometry of staggered, linked courtyards leads through individual dormitory blocks toward the education building crowning the highest mound of the gently rolling site. The dormitories and the faculty housing, already built, are remarkable in scale, at once bold (the scale of the town) and intimate (the dwelling unit). As "regional" architecture, Kahn's use of porches and his placement of buildings in accordance with the climatological information available, should be contrasted with Edward Durrell Stone's renowned United States Embassy at New Delhi of a decade ago.

Kahn's method and his shapes, especially those seemingly matter-of-fact shapes that result from what Giurgola describes as fragments of Euclidean geometry, are difficult to comprehend; and his resulting architecture is not an easy one to understand or accept; it is anticlassic, as Giurgola points out, in the same way that Palladio's is.[12] It is classic, or more accurately, classicizing, as Scully has shown, in the way it relies on that particulated compositional method which French academicians (Beaux-Arts) stressed in the early years of this century, insisting on separate spaces for separate functions and accordingly evocative.[13] "The resulting architecture," as Giurgola writes, "is not easy . . . but it comes strong and strident as all the things that are said for the first time."[14]

Kahn's finest buildings completed to date are the Eleanor Donnelley Erdman dormitories at Bryn Mawr College and the complex of laboratory buildings for the Salk Institute of Biological Studies at La Jolla, California. The dormitories are like the Richards Medical

8. Assembly Building, Dacca, East Pakistan, 1962–   View from Presidential Square. Model.

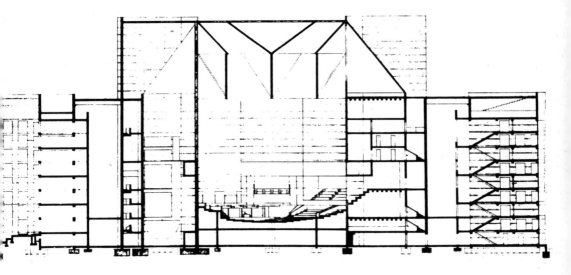

9. *Assembly Building. Cross sections of assembly room, and plan.*

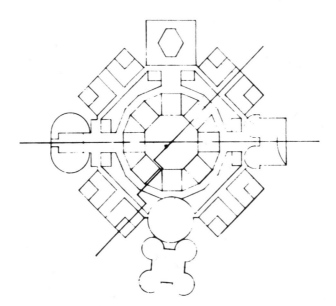

10. *Indian Institute of Management, Ahmedabad, India, 1963– . View of dormitories D 6, D 5, D 3, under construction, from northeast.*

11. *Eleanor Donnelley Erdman Dormitories, Bryn Mawr College, Bryn Mawr, Pennsylvania, 1960–65. General view.*

Research Building, a series of independent elements so arranged as to form a wall and to appear as one (*Fig. 11*). Three squares that interlock at their corners, "kissing squares" they have been called, are placed at forty-five-degree angles to the mall which they culminate. From the mall, they seem a gentle wall; from below, as Scully describes it, "a fine high palisade stretched across its military crest."[15] Gray slate panels set between thin strips of precast concrete trim recall the tough local masonry tradition which characterizes Philadelphia's residential architecture from that of Frank Furness in the 1870's and 1880's to that of George Howe in the 1920's. The internal spaces are majestic in their emptiness; yet the casually grouped, light, industrial furniture used in them is not dwarfed.

The Salk Institute is to be an academic village on a site overlooking the Pacific Ocean and will, when completed, include housing for the staff and a community center as well as extensive laboratory facilities. In the laboratories, completed in 1965, structure and services are combined in a splendid (and generously proportioned) fulfillment of Kahn's ideas about the separation and interdependence in Form of "servant" and "served" spaces (*Figs. 12–14*). The laboratory spaces are big and airy, free of columns and easily serviced from the people-sized pipe ducts. The demands of technology are

12. *Salk Institute of Biological Studies, laboratories, La Jolla, California, 1959–65. Site model from above.*

13. *Salk Institute of Biological Studies, laboratories. Lower garden.*

met at every turn, as they can only be in a complete solution to the problem. Across the hall from the laboratories, the individual studies for the scientists can be reached by stairs, and bridges lead to the open seminar spaces. Concrete is refined to a degree that has rarely revealed itself in the work of other architects: its density, its color, and its meticulously calculated joinery are remarkable, the latter the result of the insertion of teak boards between the forms to allow for expansion, a fine use of construction in the service of design.

14. *Salk Institute of Biological Studies, laboratories. Elevation of a portion of the garden facade showing concrete formwork.*

Kevin Roche

Kevin Roche, the design-partner of Roche, Dinkeloo and Associates, is the master of uncompromised geometry, carrying to exaggerated scale that reductive impulse which underlies all exclusivist architecture. The inheritor of the late Eero Saarinen's practice, and for many years his chief assistant in design, Roche shares with his former mentor a passion for strong and simple imagery. In Roche's work, this takes on a degree of abstraction and geometric purity that is quite different from Saarinen's urge to use imagery in a representational way (T.W.A. Terminal in New York City as image of flight, 1956–1962; aspirant roof profile of North Christian Church in Columbus, Indiana, 1959–1963, and so on): a tendency now being developed in the work of another of Saarinen's close associates in design, Robert Venturi. The difference between Saarinen's approach to design and that of Roche can be seen in a comparison between Saarinen's last work, the C.B.S. office building in New York City, and one of Roche's earliest independent works, the office building for the Knights of Columbus, in New Haven, now under construction.

C.B.S. is an image of quiet corporate strength (known in the broadcasting industry as "black rock"). An unbroken sweep of tower, it is supported at its perimeter by an even rhythm of closely spaced columns (*Fig. 15*). The columns, sheathed in granite, are set at angles to the facade and provide, as one views the buildings from various locations, an ever-changing pattern of open and closed, not unlike recent neoconstructivist art (also known as Op Art). A good deal in the way of functional expression is sacrificed to this system: doors at street level are confined to the spaces between the piers, thereby making the entrance virtually invisible; at the top there is no strong articulation and the building appears cut off. Saarinen's design surpasses in its reductive impulses Mies van der Rohe's Seagram Building (1958), but at the expense of vitality, even down to the insistence that the tower not be connected at its base with the low buildings which form the rest of the block, thereby denying the hierarchy of the building relationships typical of streets in Manhattan and creating useless open space at the rear.

The twenty-six-story Knights of Columbus tower has ten fewer floors than C.B.S. but the four corner towers, like turrets on some enormous medieval battlement, and the tremendous stretch of girders which connect the towers and span over twenty-four meters, make it, especially as one approaches New Haven on the highway, a rigorous statement about the power of size and of clarity in a tall building (*Fig. 16*). Only the elevators rising at the core compromise the clear imagery of the tower (and the flexibility of the interior space). The Knights of Columbus tower, not yet complete, promises resolution for some of the issues that C.B.S. does not: an integral handling of lobby entrances; a tense interplay of big-scale structure and small-scale elements of mullioning and the like; and its pure tower-profile works exceptionally well on its site, the principal vehicular entrance to the city.

Roche is also designing the adjoining New Haven Coliseum, the construction of which is expected to begin in 1969–1970 (*Figs. 17–18*). This complex building includes a garage for 2,400 cars which, carried on colossal piers, permits the fifty-six meter spans necessary to cover the arena and the exhibition hall. Beyond this bold conception, vast and undifferentiated open spaces are left along the edges of the site with no effort to adjust themselves to the scale of the city and the pedestrian.

Roche's proposal for the National Center for Higher Education at DuPont Circle in Washington, D.C., takes its shape from a recognition of the geometry of the wedge-shaped site and of the circular space it commands (*Figs. 19–20*). The unbending regularity of the horseshoe plan, though it is faithful to the geometry of the circle and provides an integral and dramatic entrance to the vast central

15. *Eero Saarinen and Associates: C.B.S. (Columbia Broadcasting System Building), Sixth Avenue and 52nd Street, New York, N.Y., 1962–64.*

16. *Kevin Roche, John Dinkeloo and Associates: Knights of Columbus Office Building, New Haven, Connecticut, to be completed 1969. General view. Composite.*

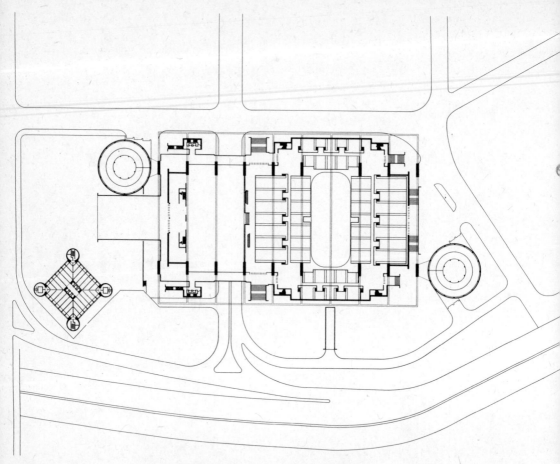

17. *Knights of Columbus Hall Office Building in relation to projected New Haven Coliseum. Plan.*

18. *New Haven Coliseum, construction to begin 1969–70. General view. Composite.*

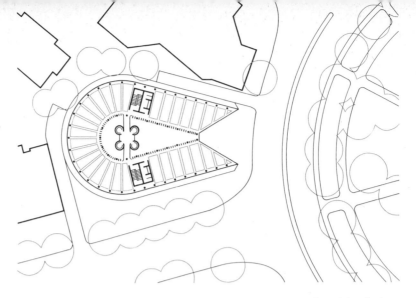

19. *National Center for Higher Education, Washington, D. C., under design. Street level plan.*

20. *National Center for Higher Education. View from DuPont Circle. Composite.*

space of the building, creates an irregular and uncharacteristic break in the wall of the street at the rear, which a more flexible (or less pure) attitude toward geometry might have avoided.

Roche's brilliance as a designer, his sure sense of proportion, his extraordinary affinity with the neoclassicism of late eighteenth-century French visionaries is nowhere more effectively seen than in a small Orangery which he designed for a large estate *(Fig. 21)*. Roche's design reflects none of the whimsy usually associated with this kind of garden structure. It is, instead, a strongly proportioned cube of masonry, with double layers of walls to accommodate retractable windows and screens. Inside, an apsoidal panel, culminating the axis of a *grande allée*, is lighted from a skylight. Equally assured, is the geometry which Roche has devised for the College Life Insurance Company *(Fig. 22)*. His most abstract conception to date, this complex of identically designed buildings on a rural site at the intersection of two important highways, looking like some lost vision

21. *Orangery, project. Perspective drawing.*

22. *College Life Insurance Company of America, Indianapolis, Indiana, to be completed 1970. View of offices. Composite.*

of Claude-Nicolas Ledoux, permits an expansion of identical amounts of office space over a period of years. Three eleven-story tapered towers will be built in the first phase. The L-shaped core for each of the buildings will be of concrete while the walls are sheathed in mirrored glass, a surface which denies the reality of the building and the functions housed within, masking individual floor heights and permitting no visual penetration of the mass. This is surely one of the most disquieting commercial images yet conceived; a great and neutral presence, full of power yet frozen.

The Oakland Museum, nearing completion, occupies a site at the edge of that city's downtown area (*Fig. 23*). Four blocks have been assembled into one to accommodate three museums. Roche's design is a "nonbuilding": from the street, the visitor sees only broad expanses of comparatively low concrete walls crowned with planting and punctuated at a few locations by entrances. Once penetrated, the wall gives way to a landscape of stepped gardens and courtyards that is at once public park, forecourt, and access to the museums. At this writing the galleries are not open to the public so it is impossible to judge the success of the museum in use. As urban design, it is a very ambitious statement and though one might question the propriety of a nonbuilding amidst Oakland's only too uneventful landscape (Oakland almost cries out for a Philip Johnson "temple"), there is no doubt that this is a work of major importance and one that strikes a serious blow for architecture at the service of city design. The design is brilliant and the end result is invaluable as a prototype for a kind of building that has a very necessary place in our architecture—one that cloaks itself in anonymity, not necessarily underground, but returning to the land its roofs and approaches. It may not be, unfortunately, the right solution to the particular problems of its site.

The Ford Foundation Headquarters in New York is Roche's most celebrated work to date (*Figs. 24–25*). Located on an unusual mid-

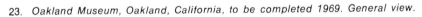

23. *Oakland Museum, Oakland, California, to be completed 1969. General view.*

block site that has a considerable change of level and is bordered along one side by a public park, the building consists of offices arranged along two sides of the site, with a covered, enclosed garden —bordering the park and Forty-second Street—occupying the remaining portion. Each office faces the enclosed courtyard, which is open to the public and serves as a pleasant pedestrian link through the block. All is exposed to the most casual passerby: the ritualistic bureacracy of private benefaction revealed in an awesome shrine.

As a work of street architecture, the Ford Foundation Building, though it respects the lines and planes of the surrounding buildings, is without scale. Because it is inward in orientation, the exterior walls are composed without reference to the sizes of openings and

24. Ford Foundation Building, 42nd Street, between First and Second Avenues, New York, N.Y., 1967.

floor levels. The great public space within—kept lush and green throughout the year, though at some considerable sacrifice to olefactory delight—does not invite repose: it is merely a landscaped passage, after all, and not a quiet sitting park. The insistent uniformity of the architecture and the conformity which the architect and the administration of this foundation impose on the staff (every ashtray, every art object, everything is selected by the architect; personal mementos, even family pictures are frowned upon), may not exactly cast doubt upon the very excellent purposes of the philanthropic enterprise itself, but do open to question the relationship between the exclusivist approach to environmental design and the messy realities of people and life.

25. *Ford Foundation Building. Interior courtyard.*

Paul Rudolph

Paul Rudolph, an architect of great ingenuity and inventiveness, has carried further the objectives of those who in the 1950's sought a way beyond the neoclassicism into which orthodox modern architecture was reverting (Lincoln Center is a good example) without breaking with the philosophical premises of orthodox modern architecture itself. Rudolph's early design, marked by an obsessive urge to give physical shape to philosophical positions, was in fact almost theory exploration at the expense of program: the Walker Guest House (minimal Miesian vocabulary in wood); Jewett Arts Center (evocation of a historical style); Sarasota High School (rationalization of Le Corbusier's work in terms of American concrete technology); Yale Art and Architecture Building (integration of Wrightian space with Corbusian form). This ability to ruthlessly pursue formal ideas made each of Rudolph's early buildings an object lesson in design at a time when very little modern architecture was being built and its scope was severely restricted to a simple set of shapes devised by Walter Gropius and Marcel Breuer in their effort to Americanize the International Style. Rudolph's rise to architectural prominence has been meteoric: looking over the entirety of his work, one is impressed by its intensity, and the boundless outpouring of talent and energy.

In contrast to Kahn's formulation of a design philosophy, Rudolph has concentrated upon questions of architectural shape. His "six determinants" of architectural form—a term he uses in the conventional sense, rather than that developed by Kahn, and referring to physical shape—include the relationship between a building and its environment, functionalism, regionalism, materials of construction, psychological demands, and the spirit of the times.[16] From these determinants emerge the formal preoccupations of his work: clear articulation and efficient use of structure; elaborate silhouettes; vertical as well as horizontal continuity of interior space; almost baroque effects of light, startling juxtapositions of opposites —open and closed spaces, rough and smooth surfaces, the man-made and the natural. These in turn give rise to a number of formal devices which Rudolph has used to great effect: the pinwheel plan, the collonade screen supporting the bold cornice, the articulated service tower, sculpted floors, floating platforms, bridges through interior spaces, inglenooks and many more. The origins of these devices are complex: some are of Rudolph's own invention but a good number are borrowed. Rudolph's eclecticism is broad, yet almost always based on the geometries developed by the leaders of the first generation of modern architects, Le Corbusier and Frank Lloyd Wright.

Rudolph was the first important designer of the second generation of modern architects in America to reject the limited historical vision of the Harvard "Bauhaus," as codified by Sigfried Giedion in

Space, Time and Architecture, and to question it openly. After traveling in Europe in 1948, he "returned to this country with the reinforced conviction of the necessity of regaining the 'form sense' which helped to shape Western man's building until the nineteenth century. Other periods have always developed means of tying their architecture to previous works without compromising their own designs. This is also our task."[17]

Rudolph's talent is that of a designer and his preoccupation with physical shape, too often at the expense of the building program, often forces him to philosophical positions of questionable wisdom. Thus, his early recognition of the limitations of the Miesian method, with its structural determinism and its neo-Platonic perfection, resulted in a plea for "an enrichment of architecture at the brink of mannerism," a statement which does much to explain such of his designs of the late 1950's as the Jewett Arts Center at Wellesley College and the Temple Street Parking Garage in New Haven.[18]

The Jewett Art Center, Rudolph's first completed commission for a large building, has become for many a notorious example of the eclectic excesses of the 1950's (*Fig. 26*). True, the use of screens, the decorative treatment of structure, and the somewhat Gothic handling of skylights and other details resemble certain confections of the decorated-box school of design associated with the work of Edward Durrell Stone and, more especially, Minoru Yamasaki. At Wellesley, however, the historical evocation of the past goes beyond a whimsical desire for architectural enrichment toward a serious recognition of the demands of urban context. Rudolph has said of the "good neighbor" policy which he pursued at Wellesley—"mood architecture," he called it—"that the danger in respecting too literally the earlier architecture, which is usually eclectic in character in this country, is that we may create a new eclecticism, i.e., one approach to creating harmony with Gothic, another to early New England, another to Georgian, etc."[19] But the harmony of scale achieved between the old and the new at Wellesley goes beyond the simple projection of a "mood," and succeeds in capturing the spirit of the past, thereby discrediting that smug hostility to the preexisting environment which had for so long stood between modern architecture and its urbanistic responsibilities.

In the Temple Street Parking Garage, the bold scale of a freeway is compressed and restricted in terms of the city street (*Fig. 27*). Though the unbending geometry of stacks of identically sized structural elements seems quite arbitrary in comparison with those of Roman aqueducts (the forms of which are distinctly recalled), a more complicated rhythm might have completely overpowered the weak shapes of the surrounding buildings. The Temple Street Garage raises as many questions as it answers. Structure and scale aside, it brings to the foreground a fundamental urban problem—how much should we invest financially and symbolically in accommodating the urban environment to the automobile? Surely we must do

26. *Mary Cooper Jewett Art Center, Wellesley College, Wellesley, Massachusetts, 1955–58. The Art Center in relation to neo-gothic Green Tower (right).*

27. *Temple Street Parking Garage, New Haven, Connecticut, 1959–62.*

something with it; but is Rudolph's answer perhaps too expensive and too prominent?

Rudolph's most complete work thus far is the Art and Architecture Building designed for Yale University (*Fig. 28*). The design of this building addresses itself to the broadest architectural issues: space, structure, services, materials, and the urban context are all scrutinized in terms of a vocabulary that goes well beyond its inspiration in Wright and Le Corbusier to become, finally, Rudolph's own. A bold composition of towers, housing mechanical services, and slabs, bridging between them, surround what was to have been a central enclosed courtyard rising continuously through the building. The fire regulations would not permit this and the evolution of the design illuminates many of the strengths and weaknesses of Rudolph's approach and ultimately that of the exclusivist method as a whole. It is now clear that the Art and Architecture Building is a functional failure because the original conception, what Kahn calls its Form, did not derive from an insight into how the building would be used, but from an abstract design idea. So many aspects of programmatic and environmental concern—light and glare control,

28. *Art and Architecture Building, Yale University, New Haven, Connecticut, 1958–63. General view.*

circulation, acoustics and privacy, even micro-climate (as anyone who has tried to ascend the front steps in winter will attest)—go unrecognized in order to satisfy a brilliant but ultimately partial vision.

The Endo Laboratories Building is, in many ways, more successful and, in its overall massing, in the disciplined handling of the curves as well as in the use of mushroom columns, the influence of Wright's Johnson Wax Company Building in Racine, Wisconsin (1936–1939, 1950), is quite clear (*Fig. 29*). Unlike Johnson Wax, which turns almost completely in upon itself, Endo (though a considerable part of it is hidden behind solid walls) appears quite open. Courtyards and ramps make gestures of invitation and provide, amidst the emptiness of the suburban Long Island landscape, a genuine place for pedestrians. At the same time the clear articulation of functional parts—lobby, cafeteria, dog run, light turrets and so on—is of sufficiently bold scale to be read by speeding motorists on the Meadowbrook Parkway a quarter of a mile away, an effective response to the twin scales of modern city life. Only the automobile, Rudolph has observed, is "large enough to organize the city on a large scale."[20]

The design for the Boston Government Center, now under construction, is the collaborative effort of a number of architectural firms working in concert under Rudolph's direction (*Fig. 30*). It is an attempt to produce a unified structure out of what was originally

29. *Endo Laboratories Building, Garden City, Long Island, New York, 1960–64. View of main entrance.*

proposed as three separate buildings occupying an irregular site near the well-known City Hall by Kallman, McKinnell and Knowles (*see Fig. 69*). The program calls for extensive, unencumbered loft space. The only fixed elements besides the structure are the mechanical services and the vertical circulation, which have been grouped in towers.

Within the Government Center the office space of the Employment Security Building and the Mental Health Building is arranged in a series of set-back terraces to break down the scale of the court and to extend its space as in an amphitheater, while the resultant arcade along the street gives it a strong definition and more monumental scale. A twenty-six-story tower rises at the end of a pedestrian street leading from the new City Hall, and gives the Sienese space of the court a focus. The use of the pinwheel configuration for the office tower is not only intended to enhance its role as a pivot at the symbolic gateway to the Government Center as a whole but also to provide, on a given floor, far greater modulation of space than would be possible in a more conventional plan shape. Combined with the "ritual circle" of columns near its core, the pinwheel begins to suggest a hierarchy of spaces with private offices along the perimeter, attached spaces for secretaries, circulation corridor and, in the center, office pools.

30. *Paul Rudolph, coordinating architect: Boston Government Center, Massachusetts, 1967– Model. Shepley, Bulfinch, Richardson and Abbott, architects: Division of Employment Security Building (left, four sections); Desmond and Lord, architects, Paul Rudolph, architectural design: Mental Health Building (above center); H.A. Dyer, Pedersen and Tilney, architects, Paul Rudolph, architectural design: Health, Welfare and Education Building (tower and slab directly behind tower).*

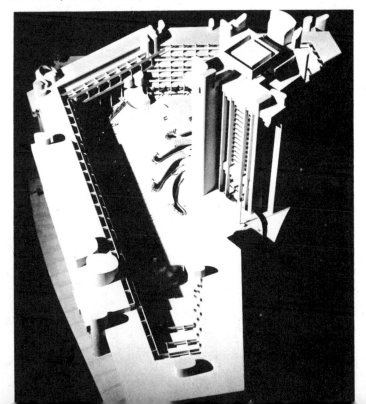

The Boston Government Center is an impressive demonstration of Rudolph's determination to see architecture extend itself beyond the provision of functional accommodation toward a true urbanity of form. Yet, at this writing, its monumentality seems overwrought; its shape, particularly as it departs from the street pattern at the corners, seems too generalized and alien to the character of Boston (though it is intimate in scale compared to the behemoths that are destroying Back Bay).

A series of projects for mass housing show Rudolph's urbanistic capabilities at a lower key and, in fact, demonstrate a concern for problem-solving that is sometimes not as evident in his more monumental commissions. Even when Rudolph has relied on building systems in his proposals for mass housing—and he has pioneered the potential use of prefabricated dwelling units built by the "mobile-homes" industry and of hung structures—his instincts as a designer and his understanding of the scale of the individual dwelling unit, have enabled him to go far beyond the sociological excuses that so many "housing architects" substitute for genuine architectural

31. *Married Student Housing, Yale University, New Haven, Connecticut, 1958–61. View of entrance.*

solutions. Within the highly restrictive demands of governmental agencies and economics, Rudolph creates *places* for people to live in; architecture, not housing.

In his designs for housing, Rudolph's qualities as a site-planner come out most clearly. Married Student Housing at Yale, a work of minimal cost and reflecting the English New Brutalism in its handling of brick and concrete (though, unlike in English work, these materials are used to sheathe a wood structure and not as structure itself), is a delightful evocation of a hillside village laid out along a broad flight of steps which function as the principal street and as a stepped plaza perfect for mothers to gather on while watching children play (*Fig. 31*).

In two projects for the first phase of the Northwest Urban Renewal Area in Washington, D.C., Rudolph, in attempting to develop an integrated system of building relating high-rise and low-rise construction, has adapted this image of a hillside village to a flat site using involved plan shapes and roofs of varied slope (*Fig. 32*). "It's my hope," Rudolph states, "that these units will seem like houses

32. *Paul Rudolph, master planner: Northwest Urban Renewal Area, Washington, D. C., 1966–* *Prince Hall. Isometric drawing.*

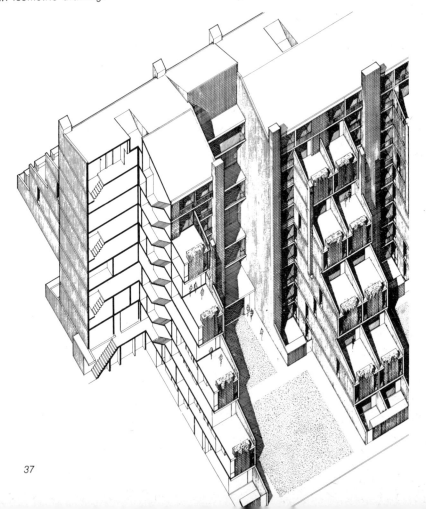

in the sky, not drawers in a cabinet."[21] Of these two projects, Golden Rule Houses tends to be overly concerned with small scale, while Prince Hall with its highly complicated plan involving terraced duplex units suggests a genuine recognition of the problems of individual identity in the modern city. The use of deep courtyards and long walls of building indicates a complete departure from Corbusian planning (the heroic, sculptured object in the landscape most beautifully fulfilled in the Unité d'Habitation at Marseilles, 1947–1951), and a return to less optimistic (in that they do not imagine a perfect dwelling unit type used in a perfect family size and so on) though more comprehensible organizing forms.

For a number of years, Rudolph has been interested in the possibilities of combining the use of suspended structures with prefabricated dwelling units based on the trailer principle to provide mass housing. Rudolph feels "that one way around the housing impasse would be to utilize ... existing prefabricated units of light

33. *Graphic Arts Center, New York, N.Y., project, 1967. Center in relation to the island. Composite.*

construction originally intended as moving units but adapted to fixed situations and transformed into architecturally acceptable living units. One approach would be to utilize vertical hollow tubes, probably rectangular in section, 40 or 50 stories in height to accommodate stairs, elevators, and mechanical services and to form a support for cantilever trusses at the top. These cantilever trusses would give a 'sky hook' from which the three dimensional unit could be hoisted into place and plugged into its vertical mechanical core. The history of architecture has often been written when the techniques intended for one phase of human activity have been adapted for another."[22]

Rudolph's design for the Graphic Arts Center at the tip of Manhattan Island is a fantastic complex providing 4,000 dwelling units clustered about twenty-six service cores, with vast spaces for industry provided in a stepped base (*Figs. 33–34*). Rudolph's proposal includes the use of prefabricated units built by the mobile-

34. *Graphic Arts Center. Pinwheel arrangement of prefabricated dwelling units. Model from above.*

homes industry according to his own design. The dwelling units, capsules in effect, are arranged in pinwheel fashion around the masts—"one of the good things about a pinwheel," Rudolph states, "is that it hides the repetitive nature of the building"—so that the roof of a lower unit can serve as a terrace for the one above.[23]

Rudolph's plan is the most ambitious project to result from the attention that the Lower Manhattan Plan (designed by Conklin and Rossant, Wallace, McHarg and Todd for The City of New York in 1966) has focused on a once neglected portion of the city. The design, dazzling though it is in many respects, especially in its use of structure and its multidirectional organization of functions, re-grettably projects a massive bulk along the shore that would prob-ably intensify the sense of separation from the water that many New Yorkers already feel. (The project will not be built.)

The Graphic Arts Center should be contrasted with Waterside, a smaller project designed by Davis, Brody and Associates, and soon to be constructed (*Fig. 35*). Though less dazzling in conception and quite unrelated to technological innovation, Waterside goes beyond Rudolph's proposal in one major respect: its relationship to the water. Built on a platform over the East River, it not only creates a new housing resource but also a new land resource, a large public plaza on three levels which cascade down to the river's edge. This plaza

35. *Davis, Brody and Associates: Waterside Apartments, East River Drive, between 25th and 30th Streets, Manhattan, New York, under design. Perspective drawing.*

will not only serve the residents of Waterside but also the city itself (there will be restaurants, an ice-skating rink, and two theaters), being the only public plaza directly at the river's edge along the whole of Manhattan Island and being immediately accessible and relatively apparent from upland positions. The forms of the towers themselves, a recognition of the diversity of possible apartment layouts and of the greater desirability of units atop a tower with so sweeping a view, also reflect a recognition of the inherent vitality of the apartment house vernacular with its wonderful landscape of setbacks that flowered in New York City in the middle fifties and which was virtually killed by the zoning ordinance of 1961.

Another of Rudolph's projects using the mobile-home principle was carried much closer to realization than the Graphic Arts Center. A scheme for housing married students at the University of Virginia, it proposed an all-wood-stressed skin prototype for the kind of units contemplated for the bigger project (*Fig. 36*). The Married Student Housing design was rejected by Charlottesville officials as being inappropriate, and one is inclined to agree that, insofar as the ground plane is left free and the pinwheeled grouping of the buildings is relatively directionless, the urbanistic implications of the scheme are in some ways less attractive than the clarity of the ordinary garden apartment alternative.

36. *Married Student Housing, the University of Virginia, Charlottesville, Virginia, project, 1967. Perspective drawing.*

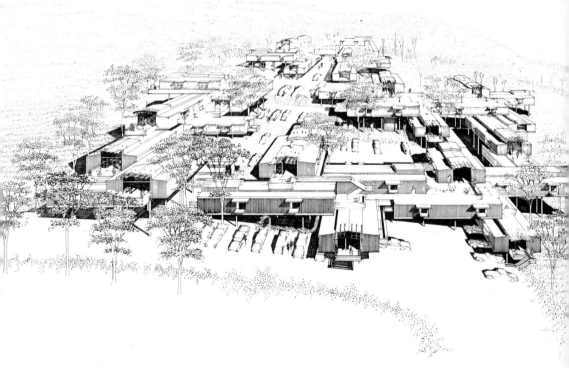

Philip Johnson

Philip Johnson is above all an intelligent architect. "At his best, he is," as Scully has put it, "admirably lucid, unsentimental, and abstract, with the most ruthlessly aristocratic, highly studied taste of anyone practicing in America today. All that nervous sensibility, lively intelligence, and a stored mind can do, he does."[24] His evolution in design reflects, in the best sense of that word, the evolution of the exclusivist position: first as a critic, giving America a formalist interpretation of the modern architecture of the 1920's—dubbed, if not by him, at least under the spell of his enthusiasm, "The International Style"[25]; then as an architect and polemicist, making Mies's work known and felt by all architects; and now, tirelessly searching for a way beyond Miesian design that, for Johnson, must finally be Miesian in conception if not in detail. Mies has given Johnson a way of doing things, a set of codified details. His is the way of orthodox modern architecture: a building, the box of space, the skin of glass, the highly edited structural expression. These can be seen as the ingredients of a universal architecture which, universally applicable though it may be, solves very few real problems, permitting them to solve themselves, instead, within a vast loftlike environment that is flexible to the point of anonymity.

Johnson is a functionalist, as Rudolph is not. His buildings always work, more often, in exclusivist fashion, because he has not gone beyond the design of universal spaces in which other people, architects or so-called space designers, work out specific solutions. Johnson is a formalist as well, but his buildings seldom go beyond the packaging of functions toward that kind of insistent interpenetration and relatedness of parts, that breathless and wrought-up quality which characterizes Rudolph's design. Johnson's approach to design has always been an urban one; the eclecticism of his shapes, no matter how eccentric, and even excessive, is always rendered insignificant by his exact sense of siting and his ability to organize complex programs in a clear manner. Though Rudolph is the most inventive of the excluding architects, Johnson is the most articulate, both with words and forms, carrying to an extreme of diagrammatic clarity the reductive and especially the selective impulses that characterize the exclusive approach.

Johnson's response to problems of urban design, characteristically, is not one of adjusting new buildings to old, but of concern for their sequential arrangement. "Architecture," he has written, "is surely *not* the design of space, certainly not the massing or organizing of volumes. These are auxiliary to the main point which is the organization of procession. Architecture exists only in *time*. . . . The whence and whither is primary. Now almost secondary is all our ordinary work, our work on forms, our plans, our elevations."[26]

The famous Glass House and subsequent outbuildings which Johnson has built for his own use in New Canaan, Connecticut, con-

37. *Philip Johnson: The architect's house (Glass House) and out buildings, New Canaan, Connecticut, 1949–65. Site plan: 1. Glass House, 2. Brick Guest House, 3. Pavilion, 4. Underground Art Gallery.*

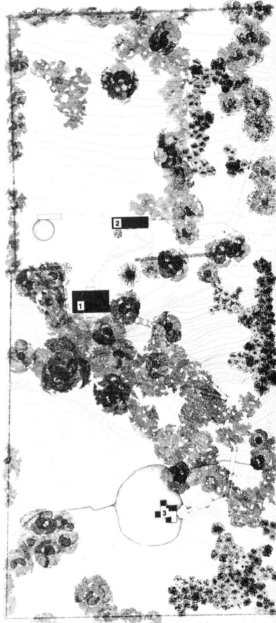

stitute a major source for studying the evolution of his design (*Figs. 37–38*). More importantly, they form the most complex and successful grouping of exclusivist buildings anywhere and have been amply discussed, especially by Johnson himself. Taken as a whole, they can be seen as a microcosm of the best that exclusivist architecture can do at the scale of town planning: closed, uninflected, separate structures, carefully positioned along a "processional" route, far enough apart to be viewed, each on its own terms, yet sometimes making outdoor spaces of considerable force.[27]

In 1963–1965 an existing pond was vastly expanded, a pavilion built at its edge (*Fig. 39*), and a path and bridge (to connect it, in straight runs, uphill to the Glass House) have been built as has an "underground" art gallery (really a building set into the side of an extended and rounded hill; *Figs. 40–42*). These have all expanded the processional possibilities of the place and the ritual of movement from one building and function to another. The gallery, composed of intersecting circles of unequal radii, goes beyond Johnson's usually rigid neoclassicism toward rich spatial statement. Its principal room, the walls of which are the diameters of the circles, is a kind of anti-space, remarkably appropriate to the work of avant-garde artists which it displays and perhaps the only gallery space yet built that is.

Even in Johnson's most distressingly decorative work, the sense of expressive functional organization along a route of movement is never lost. The siting of the Amon Carter Museum in Fort Worth culminates a long mall—which extends the impact of the building to the scale of all the city—without forcing the visitor to traverse its length before entering. The siting is an excellent example of Johnson's skills as an urban designer in triumph over an eclecticism of architectural shape (*Fig. 43*). So too, the New York State Theatre, in which the sequence of movement from plaza to ticket office to theatre and to promenade space (the lobby) is the only completely successful spatial sequence in all of Lincoln Center and can be acknowledged by even those who find Johnson's "Mississippi Promenade," with its "silhouetted moving people who form the living friezes to the space," more a gold plated jail (*Fig. 44*).

A recently completed complex of buildings, the Kline Science Center at Yale University, crowns a gentle knoll on the edge of Yale's campus known as Pierson-Sage Square (*Fig. 45*). At the edge of the site, and well below the crown of the hill, neo-Gothic buildings of the twenties and thirties line Prospect Street, while just to the side of the principal axis of Hillhouse Avenue, the Gibbs Laboratory, a modern building of the 1950's, forms a wall for the open space. Though Eero Saarinen had originally proposed that a building straddle the axis of Hillhouse Avenue, Johnson has permitted the axis to continue, siting a tall slab to one side and connecting it to Gibbs with a pergola. "What I intend . . . is space seen in motion," Johnson has written, "A walk with changes in direction with changing

38. *Glass House and Brick Guest House, 1949. General view.*

39. *Pavilion and bridge in relation to Glass House, 1963–65.*

40. *Underground Art Gallery, 1964–65. Exterior view.*

41. *Underground Art Gallery. Interior plan.*

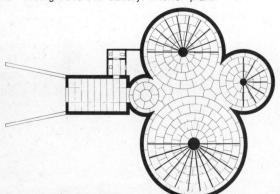

42. *Underground Art Gallery. Interior view.*

objectives. Also a slipping by of people . . . like the diagonal walkings on the Seagram Plaza. Primary to this is clarity . . . Walking up the hill at the upper end of Hillhouse, you enter through a propylaeum, a covered, columned portico. To the right the bastion of Gibbs; straight ahead—nothing. . . . Before you a paved square. . . . Dominating your view is, however, immediately to your left, the Tower with its 100-foot wide entrance steps. . . . Before you enter the Tower, you note at the north, or right of it, a grove of young trees, shade, green in the summer, twiggy in the winter. . . . Basically, the position of the Tower itself should clarify since it is strongly axial north and south. The Tower and the base of the Tower are *both* always visible. Inside the building, whether you enter from the front or the rear, you enter into the foyer facing the plaza, with the plaza on one side of the long hall, the elevators on the other. With the entering of the elevator, all processional is lost; it is the end of a chapter of architecture."[28]

The John F. Kennedy Memorial at Dallas carries to the most extreme and lyric, that reductive urge which characterizes exclusivist architecture (*Fig. 46*). Here the need to mark a horrible event is quietly met by Johnson, with little more than a courtyard, the walls of which are slightly raised above the ground, an expression not of the fullness of life but of the emptiness of violent death.

43. *Amon Carter Museum of Western Art, Fort Worth, Texas, 1961. General view.*

44. *Philip Johnson and Richard Foster: New York State Theatre, Lincoln Center for the Performing Arts, New York, N.Y., 1964. View of promenade.*

45. *Philip Johnson and Richard Foster: Kline Science Center, Yale University, New Haven, Connecticut, 1962. General view.*

46. *John F. Kennedy Memorial, Dallas, Texas, project, 1965. Model.*

Robert Venturi

Robert Venturi, Davenport Professor of Architecture at Yale University, is the chief advocate of the inclusive approach, leading to what he describes as the "difficult order," wherein all levels of problems, and all solutions, internal (functional and structural) as well as external (environmental), are considered as one. A building is held to be but a portion and an extension of its environment and a response to its location, with the outer walls no longer just a curtain or an envelope, or even a mere expression of inner functions, but a resolution of the needs of internal and external program.

More than any other architect of his generation, Venturi understands, as Donlyn Lyndon has written, "what it is like actually to look at things."[29] This he owes in part to the influence of Jean Labatut, a distinguished teacher at Princeton's architecture school, and a man who has devoted himself to the revitalization of Beaux-Arts *principles* in terms of modern needs.

Venturi's buildings grow from a deep commitment to the landscape. In the early 1950's, when American architects were just beginning to turn to the generation of Mies—and to compare it, in turn, to that of Alberti and Vignola—Venturi had already recognized the limitations of the neoclassical method as well as the antiurbanism which underlay much of the thinking of the leaders of the International Style. In an article on the changing relationship through history between Michelangelo's Campidoglio and its urban context, Venturi wrote what has become for him a guiding principle: "The architect has a responsibility toward the landscape, which he can subtly enhance or impair, for we see in perceptual wholes and the introduction of any new building will change the character of all the other elements in a scene."[30]

Venturi proposes an architecture that accepts the actual conditions of a building: the grubby limitations of economics and function. Rejecting the reductive goals of orthodox modern architecture, he proposes a new urbanism, bending program and technology to the demands of place. He does not reject the idea of a modern architecture but is concerned with revitalizing the genuine traditions and principles of a modern architecture in terms of mid-century programs just as Le Corbusier was concerned with reorienting the architecture of the twenties in terms of the vital issues of that day. Le Corbusier turned toward the industrial landscape for inspiration (industrial buildings take their shape as a result of inner uses); Venturi looks toward the landscape of the commercial "strip" (which takes its shape from external as well as internal pressures). In accepting the commercial strip, Venturi returns to an earlier and recently discredited architectural tradition in which buildings achieve symbolic effect through iconological means rather than abstract ones (as contrasted by the difference between a Gothic cathedral and a Greek temple).

Venturi and his partner, John Rauch, have recently entered a number of competitions besides that for housing at Brighton Beach, which I have already touched on. The firm's submissions to these competitions are what Venturi describes as "hybrids": "Our scheme for the F.D.R. Memorial, was architecture *and* landscape; our fountain for the Philadelphia Fairmount Park Commission, was architecture *and* sculpture; our design for Copley Plaza, architecture *and* urban design ... [while that for] the National Football Hall of Fame, is a building and a billboard."[31]

The F.D.R. competition, the earliest and most important of these contests, was marred by the inability of most of the competitors (and the jurors) to get beyond mere architecture and/or sculpture to an essential understanding of a monument in that place, its purpose, and the means by which it would be experienced (*Fig. 47*). Venturi's project, as Donlyn Lyndon has written, was the "only one which made sensible use of the automobile experience of Washington, making the tour road itself a part of the monument ... [breaking] down the normal division between building and road, monument and playground, landform and structure. It is at once a simple and quiet addition to the total landscape."[32] In accepting the scale of the road and refusing to be a fourth sculptural form next to a parking lot, the project does not reject the sidewalk and the plaza but offers, instead, opportunities for different experiences, permitting the motorist to stop, get out from behind his machine, penetrate a great wall and descend gentle steps to a great marble terrace along the Potomac. Venturi's scheme received an honorable mention. The winning scheme, the well-known *stele* designed by Pedersen and Tilney, architects, Beer, Wasserman and Hoberman, associate architects, was rejected by the Roosevelt family and will not be built. Nor is it likely that Marcel Breuer's subsequent, and similar design, approved by the Roosevelt family but criticized by the Fine Arts Commission, will be built either.

This concern with the multiplicity of scales in design informs Venturi's other proposals for civic monuments. The Fairmount Park Fountain, Philadelphia, set on an island in the middle of the Benjamin Franklin Parkway that already contains a circular Information Center,

47. *Venturi and Rauch, George Patton and Nicholas Gianopulos: Competition entry for F. D. R. Memorial along tidal basin embankment, Washington, D. C., honorable mention, 1960. Section perspective.*

48. *Venturi and Rauch, Denise Scott Brown: Fountain Competition entry for Philadelphia Fairmount Park Art Association, Philadelphia, Pennsylvania, project, 1964. View toward Art Museum. Composite.*

49. *Venturi and Rauch, Gerod Clark and Arthur Jones: Entry for Copley Square Competition, Boston, Massachusetts, project, 1966. Composite sections and plan.*

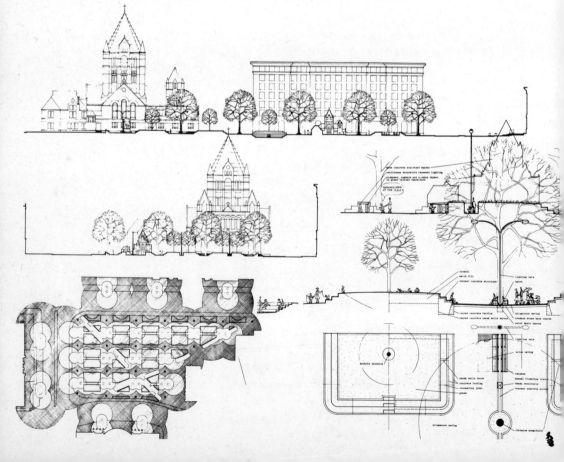

occupies a pivotal location on axis with the tower of the City Hall as well as with the central pediment of the Art Museum about a mile away (*Fig. 48*). The shape of the fountain is determined by the environment. Its boldness is necessary to give it impact in its vast and amorphous setting, its incomplete shape is a grotto sheltering the water, receiving the thrust of the Parkway and giving it direction at the scale of the moving automobile.

The project for Copley Square, Boston, accepts the likelihood of change around it and the general unrelatedness of the boundary buildings (*Fig. 49*). It is in spirit quite close to Kevin Roche's Oakland Museum, though the Boston site seems more appropriate to the idea. That is to say, it is a nonbuilding, in this case as Venturi writes, a "non-piazza ... [filling] up the space to define the space.... The traditional piazza is for collective use as well as individual use and public ceremonies involving crowds are even harder to imagine in Copley Square than passeggiate. Our square therefore is not an open space to accommodate non-existing crowds (empty piazzas are intriguing only in early de Chiricos), but to accommodate the individual who comfortably walks through the maze and sits along the 'streets' rather than in a 'piazza.' "[33]

The proposal for the National Football Hall of Fame (a scheme entered in competition for the commission) is for a building of some civic importance, one which, however, will be sited in an exploded landscape of parked automobiles (*Figs. 50–51*). It combines tra-

50. *Venturi and Rauch, Gerod Clark: Entry for National Football Hall of Fame Competition, New Brunswick, New Jersey, project, 1967. Model.*

51. *National Football Hall of Fame. Interior of main hall. Composite.*

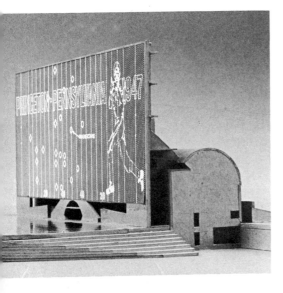

ditional architectural elements and compositional devices with those of the commercial vernacular: "You just can't see space, form and structure across a teaming parking lot without a mixture of other media. Our mixed media include ... symbolic and representational elements, that is billboards and words, along with the abstract elements of space, form and structure. Symbols with architecture enrich meaning. They can evoke the instant associations crucial for today's vast spaces, fast speeds, complex programs and, perhaps, jaded senses which respond only to bold stimuli."[34]

Venturi's first design for a projected office building for Transportation Square in the Southwest Urban Renewal Area in Washington, D.C. (this was a competition which he won; (*Figs. 52–53*),

52. *Caudill Rowlett Scott, Venturi and Rauch, associated architects: First-prize entry in 1968 competition for Transportation Square, Southwest Urban Renewal Area, Washington, D. C., under design. Site plan.*

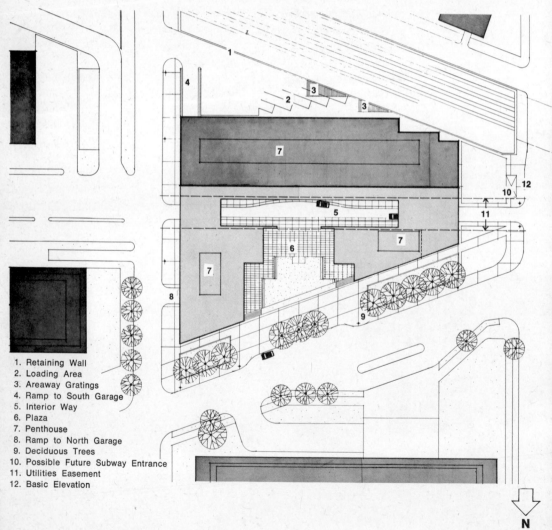

1. Retaining Wall
2. Loading Area
3. Areaway Gratings
4. Ramp to South Garage
5. Interior Way
6. Plaza
7. Penthouse
8. Ramp to North Garage
9. Deciduous Trees
10. Possible Future Subway Entrance
11. Utilities Easement
12. Basic Elevation

N

can be considered in relation to early works of the International Style, especially to Le Corbusier's design for the Palace of the League of Nations in Geneva (1927) and to Alvar Aalto's more recent Pension Bank Building in Helsinki (1952–1956). A complex form, it is a slab and at the same time defines a courtyard; it is monumental —in the forced perspective of the principal courtyard—and matter-of-fact in the cross-axial commercial strip that takes advantage of a required utility easement to provide a vital street context for the buildings at the base of the slab; it is blandly "monumental" in the manner of Washington's government office buildings though it is intricately composed as they are not, utilizing a complex spatial module. Venturi's proposal should be contrasted with Roche's design

53. *Transportation Square. Above, view toward Capital; below, view along interior way.*

for the Ford Foundation (*see Figs. 24–25*) where the big scale and small scale, filing cabinet and suburban garden, are treated with minimum contrast, yielding easier, and more legible, results. Venturi and the associated architects are now revising the design to meet certain objections from the Fine Arts Commission.

Guild House, apartments for the elderly in Philadelphia, is Venturi's biggest building completed to date and his most complex (*Figs. 54–55*). It uses conventional elements in unconventional ways, yielding a double reading: a subtle relationship between context and ideal. Charles W. Moore's analysis suggests the importance of this building in relation to the goals of inclusivist architects: Guild House "calls at once upon the intricacies of apartment floor planning of the 1920's and the simple palette of materials of 19th century Philadelphia to which is added a kind of commercial formalism with a row of white subway tile which makes a gesture toward the grandest kind of historic composition—making, dividing the whole big lump of a building into base (of white tiles), shaft (of brick) and capital (of brick, as well, but divided from the shaft by the course of white tile) without ever departing from homely matter-of-factness, so that a gold anodized television antenna on the pediment above the entrance provides a sculptural flourish at once fiercely ingenious and pathetic (we know how cheap they are). Directly below this flourish the conflicting requirements of entrance and central support fight it out. Behind it, on the back, the unadorned bricks and apparently regular holes state confidently that this is an ordinary housing project."[35]

Venturi's projected complex of buildings for the center of North Canton, Ohio, grew out of a typical need to revitalize the decaying core of a small American town (*Figs. 56–58*). Venturi's work is part of a larger plan prepared by planning consultants for the renewal of the entire downtown area. The proposal is distinguished in two respects: as a piece of urban design, relating diverse buildings, new, existing, and remodeled, to each other in a manner that is appropriate to the scale of Main Street (and is not a reincarnation of some romanticized vision of urban splendor, as are Reston and Stafford Harbor; *see Figs.* 115, 119) and for the design of the individual buildings, upon which the success of the overall plan depends.

The Town Hall is a freestanding building which crowns the axis of the central square across the street (*Fig. 57*). From afar this affords an approach to the building that is monumental and ceremonial; while from close-up, along the street (which is the way people approach on an everyday basis), one that is much more casual. The Town Hall is, as Venturi has stated, "like a Roman temple in its general proportions—in contrast with a Greek temple —a directional building whose front is more important than its back." A bold arch is swung across the facade, reflecting Sullivan's use of a similar device to give "image, unity and monumental scale" to

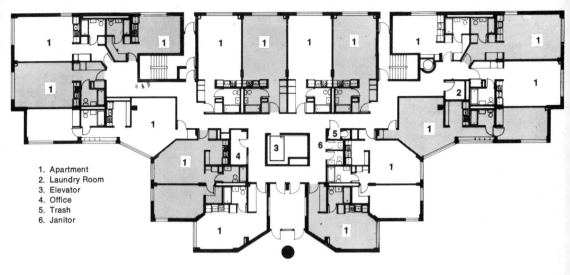

1. Apartment
2. Laundry Room
3. Elevator
4. Office
5. Trash
6. Janitor

54. *Venturi and Rauch, Cope & Lippincott, associated architects: Guild House, Friends Housing for the Elderly, Philadelphia, Pennsylvania, 1960–65. Plan of first floor.*

55. *Guild House. General view.*

56. *Venturi and Rauch for Clarke & Rapuano, Inc.: Four buildings for the center of North Canton, Ohio, 1965. Site model: Town Hall (upper right), Y.M.C.A. (lower left), public library (lower right), commercial development (above center).*

57. *North Canton. Perspective drawing of Town Hall (right) in relation to Y.M.C.A. (left).*

many of his small town banks, which "are important but small buildings on the main streets of mid-Western towns." The front of the building houses the ceremonial functions of the program, which are unlikely to change or expand. It is like the false fronts of buildings in Western towns, acknowledging the context of the street while intensifying the symbolic role of the building in the life of the town. ("The enormous flag is perpendicular to the street so that it reads from up the street like a commercial sign.")[36] The routine offices for the administrative departments are housed in a bland box at the rear of the building, which is capable of continual reorganization within and expansion should it be needed (it is in effect, a Miesian universal space).

The Y.M.C.A. Building performs quite a different function in the townscape (*Fig. 58*). Its complicated plan reflects the intricate program as it is accommodated to a sloping site with a ceremonial front along a square and a working front along a parking lot on the other side. A screen wall is employed along the plaza front to simplify the openings and make them bigger; this is intended to help to relate the "Y" to the much bigger factory building across the square; along the back the facade reflects the complexities within. The space between the screen wall and the building itself is a buffer which, because of the contours of the site, acts as a great ramp focusing on an existing church on Main Street.

The library is a remodeling, or more properly, an addition, wrapped around an entirely conventional provincial modern building of the early 1950's. The same screening device used in the "Y," in the library juxtaposes the new and old architecture and lends definition to the street.

58. *North Canton, Y.M.C.A. Elevation.*

Romaldo Giurgola

Romaldo Giurgola's is a more expansive and less intense talent than Venturi's or Kahn's, from which it has drawn so much sustenance. An Italian by birth and early education, his is a sensibility that sketches with soft lines and gently shaded areas (in contrast to the intense intricacy of Rudolph's linear technique or Venturi's concise, informational approach).

Giurgola, who is Chairman of the Department of Architecture at Columbia University, has written beautifully about the city, describing it as "a complex of poetic essence" and pointing out the fallacy of theory elaboration in modern city planning. "Too often a theory or a competent principle counts more in essence than in realization. Results derived from preconceived positions are identifiable in high schematization of plans; in pedantic separation of traffic routes; in definite specialization of areas, boundaries; in presumptious formalism of symbolic areas—all of which reduce design to a search for evidence of predetermined theories. This search transforms the urban organism into a demonstration and in consequence kills it, in destroying the human phenomena within it. The search destroys the very idea of a city, and, too often, it makes the architecture an end in itself rather than a means.

"Yet we should work with the ideas of a city rather than a theory of it. The very human phenomena with which the theoreticians deal remain relevant facts of a city—facts that are inherently opposed to simplification and forced clarification of programs. Human phenomena—the exaltation of complexities, infinite possibilities, imponderables—cannot be reduced to statistics. Order must not be confused with theory elaboration and its consequences: visual formalism. Order comes, rather, from a realistic apprehension of the facts that make the city—facts that extend from the historical experience of human events to the functional logic of its structures."[37] Giurgola rejects the notion of movement systems as the essence of the modern city. In his second-prize entry in the town-planning competition for Tel Aviv-Yafo, which he prepared in association with his partner, Ehrmann B. Mitchell, Jr., and a team including David Crane and Thomas R. Vreeland, Jr., the core of a revitalized Tel Aviv was seen as a "city of ideas and leisure."[38] A linear organization, a kind of extended core, is proposed to define a "super space" within which a series of pedestrian ways provide strong links to the water where apartment slabs step up to emphasize the expanse of sea and sky (Fig. 59).

Giurgola's most satisfying works are often his most modest. The student dormitory buildings for the Academy of the New Church at Bryn Athyn, uses the Brutalist vocabulary of brick-bearing walls and concrete lintels in a long rectangular block, grouping common spaces on one side facing the campus and bedroom spaces on the other facing the open country (Fig. 60). The apparent simplicity of the

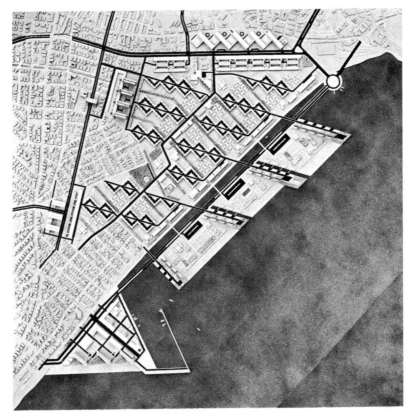

59. *Mitchell/Giurgola Associates: Second-prize entry, competition for Tel Aviv-Yafo, Israel, 1963. Site plan.*

60. *Student dormitory buildings, Academy of the New Church, Bryn Athyn, Pennsylvania, 1963. General view.*

dormitories is deceptive. Within the overall shape there is extensive modulation of individual room units, a courtyard for the master's apartment, use of skylights to define common spaces and to establish a visual link between the campus and the corridor.

In a "vest-pocket" infill addition to the Philadelphia Life Insurance Company offices, on Broad Street, just north of City Hall, Giurgola devised a facade that is obvious, as such, and related in scale to the existing building though not wholly dependent upon it (*Fig. 61*). Glass is set flush with the stone front in the large panes and deeply recessed in the strips to emphasize the planarity of the masonry and suggest a tautness of composition quite lacking in the weaker design of the older building.

61. *Philadelphia Life Insurance Company Building, Broad Street, Philadelphia, Pennsylvania, 1962. General view.*

The residence for Mrs. Thomas White in Chestnut Hill is a cubist composition of volumes that appears to be completely casual (and in this respect is in marked contrast to the wrought-up cubism of younger architects). The use of a diagonal, so intensely exploited by Kahn and Venturi as an expression of sudden spatial shift, becomes much less urgent, suggesting merely a corner bay window (*Fig. 62*).

The distorted geometry of the National Park Headquarters Building in Bar Harbor, on Mt. Desert Island, Maine, resulted from Giurgola's desire to have the building culminate the rising landscape and become a viewing platform above the level of the trees without becoming an object for contemplation (*Figs. 63–64*). Deck and roof are ambiguously interrelated to minimize the disruptive impact of the building on the land, though the projected use of reinforced concrete construction and glazed-ochre roof tiles does not seem completely sympathetic.

In a competition for International House, Philadelphia, a residence for four hundred students, Giurgola projected six houses organized around a courtyard used for games (*Figs. 65–66*). An ingenious dwelling unit incorporating four bedrooms on two levels, with a living room halfway between, forms the basic component. Here the use of a diagonal to expand the space of the living room and contain that of the bedrooms is more integral than at the house for Mrs. White. Giurgola writes, "The living spaces of the suites face

62. *Residence for Mrs. Thomas White, Chestnut Hill, Philadelphia, Pennsylvania, 1963. General view.*

onto the courtyard: a parade of houses in a square, like a city, facing toward the University."[39] The entrance to the courtyard is on the diagonal and at the corner, leading past the specialized apartments and separate from entrances to the residential houses themselves, making the courtyard space an extension of street and yet a private place.

Giurgola's second-prize submission to the Boston City Hall competition, designed in association with Thomas R. Vreeland, Jr., has proved more influential than that of the winning entry by Kallmann, McKinnell and Knowles, now built (*cf. Figs. 67–68, 69*). Whereas the winning scheme is an excellent summation of design preoccupations of the early sixties, with the big, bold sculptural shapes, expressing

63. *National Park Headquarters, Mt. Desert Island, Maine, project, 1965. Model.*

64. *National Park Headquarters. Section.*

the principal ceremonial functions of government, packaged within a closed form, Giurgola's scheme seems to prefigure developments in the attitude toward shape and urban design only now beginning to manifest themselves widely: it is an open-ended scheme, a complex image, with an office building surrounding a court on three sides and a separate building for the ceremonial functions. The council chamber is lit by an elaborate cupola which resolves the differing heights of the two buildings and relates, on a twentieth-century scale, to the lanterns and cupolas on various older buildings in the immediate vicinity.

Thus, in Giurgola's scheme, the City Hall is both a relatively small building housing mayor and council (related to Faneuil Hall and

65. *Entry invited in competition for International House, Philadelphia, Pennsylvania, project, 1965. Model.*

66. *International House. Floor plans.*

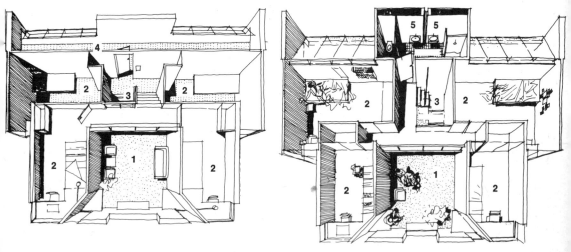

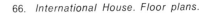

Living Room   2. Bedroom   3. Entrance   4. Corridor   5. Bathroom

67. *Mitchell/Giurgola Associates and Thomas R. Vreeland, Jr.: Second-prize entry, competition for Boston City Hall, Massachusetts, 1962. Site plan.*

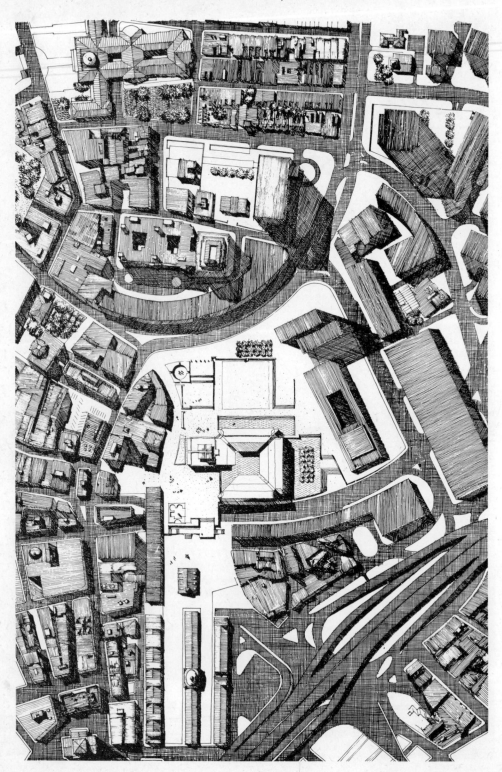

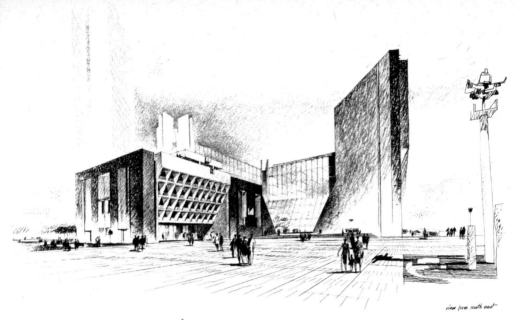

68. *Boston City Hall. Perspective Drawing of City Hall from Southwest.*

69. *Kallmann, McKinnell, and Knowles: First-prize entry, competition for Boston City Hall, Massachusetts, to be completed 1969. General view.*

to the scale of the markets and the waterfront beyond) and a giant office building (related in scale to a huge complex of other government and commercial buildings which it is physically and functionally a part of). Neither the winning scheme nor Giurgola's is a simple object in space, as the overall urban design concept within which the competitors were asked to work seemed to imply, and as the majority of the entries in the competition were. But in the second-prize winner, much more than in the first, one can measure a gathering up of the forces of all the buildings at that place, the creation of a building that is a complex articulation of a complex program, legible in its organization and completely unsentimental in its recognition of the twin aspects of city government: bureaucracy and symbol.

The fate at the hands of the Capital Fine Arts Commission of Giurgola's design selected in competition for the American Institute

70. *First-prize entry, competition for A.I.A. (American Institute of Architects) Headquarters, Washington, D. C., 1965. Model.*

of Architects in Washington, D.C., underscores the conflict between the inclusive and exclusive attitudes (*Figs. 70–71*). Willis N. Mills, Chairman of the A.I.A. Headquarters Committee, implied as much when he stated his belief that the disagreement arises "from the basic approach to the problem. Mitchell-Giurgola sees this as a challenge to mix the new and the old with proper respect for each. They therefore seek to create a 'place' in Giurgola's term, a single composition where the form of the new building finds its genesis and inspiration in the old. Both are related in a powerful manner to the central garden which becomes the focus of each. . . . The Fine Arts Commission, on the other hand, takes the position of a preservationist. Here is an important building in its Georgian garden. It is a pleasant, tranquil spot, which should not be disturbed. Therefore, anything that intrudes should go away."[40] Giurgola, having had three designs for the headquarters rejected by the Arts Commission, has now resigned.

71. *Final (third) submission, A.I.A. Headquarters, 1968. Model.*

Charles W. Moore

Charles W. Moore has until recently been associated in practice and in the formulation of his ideas with Donlyn Lyndon, William Turnbull, and Richard Whitaker. Now, Lyndon is Dean of Architecture at M.I.T.; Whitaker is working for the A.I.A., and Turnbull and Moore are in partnership. Like Venturi, Moore, Lyndon and Turnbull are graduates of Princeton where, Lyndon writes, "many of their most fundamental convictions were formed. . . ." From Jean Labatut, they "learned to see, from Kahn [who was at that time lecturing at Princeton as was Venturi] to seek a general encompassing order" and from Enrico Peressutti, an Italian architect then very influential at Princeton, they learned to experience "the fervour and delight of shaping specific forms to the discipline of circumstance."[41]

Moore and his associates have adopted the "proposition . . . that the first purpose of architecture is territorial, that the architect sets out the stimuli with which the observer creates an image of 'place.' The architect particularizes. . . ." By directing factors of functional accommodation "to a controlling image, he is building the opportunity for people to know where they are—in space, in time and in the order of things. He gives them something to be in. . . . In working we do not reject games, postures or the apparently arbitrary fancies and associations of those for whom we build, but rather seek to fashion from these a sensible order that will extend our own, and our users', ability to perceive and assimilate the delights and complexities of an untheoretical world. To build such places, often on a low budget, we like to, and must, build simply with readily available techniques."[42] This attitude revels in the idiosyncracy of use as it modifies form, and can be seen as a manifestation of Erich Fromm's life-loving principle. It is antithetic to the exclusivist attitude which might be seen as the love of things, especially in their perfect state, or, to rely on Fromm's terms, "the attraction to what is not alive (dead or mechanical)." It is also as much a reflection of what Moore and the others, Lyndon writes, "disavow as by what we profess. We do not believe that each problem is a specific instance of a general case, that the first task of architecture is shelter, nor that the greatest task is clarification of structure."[43]

While associated with the firm of Clarke and Beuttler, Moore designed an extension to the Citizen's Federal Savings & Loan Association on Market Street in San Francisco, in which the character of the old building is maintained and the difficult corner is filled and turned in a way that the countless corner buildings in Haussmann's Paris are (*Fig. 72*). It is, together with Skidmore, Owings & Merrill's John Hancock Life Insurance Building of 1959, the only new high-rise construction to work with the gentle character of San Francisco rather than to inject a kind of transplanted Miesian design via Chicago.

In the middle sixties, Moore, together with his partners produced a series of crotchety shacklike cottages akin to the indigenous architecture of the San Francisco Bay Region, yet revealing a disciplined geometry quite unlike that area's usual random character. In Moore's own cottage at Orinda, two distorted pyramidical canopies, each supported on four posts, are asymmetrically juxtaposed within a larger roof of similar shape and similar distortion (*Figs. 73–74*). This is in contrast to Philip Johnson's own house, where a virtually identical program (a bachelor architect's residence) is restricted to the confines of a box and given spatial expression through the placement of furniture (see *Fig. 37*).

Sea Ranch, a residential resort development about three hours' drive north of San Francisco, is a significant demonstration of the urbanistic capabilities of Moore's interpretation of shack-style architecture. Sea Ranch goes beyond mere new-town housing to project

72. *Charles W. Moore, Clark and Beuttler: Extension to Citizen's Federal Savings & Loan Association, Kearny and Market Streets, San Francisco, California, 1962. General view.*

73. *Charles W. Moore: The architect's house at Orinda, California, 1961. Exterior view.*

74. *The architect's house at Orinda. Interior.*

a unified image. Like the harmonic composition of preindustrial towns, it speaks of the willingness of many to give up something for the community.

The project is the result of close collaboration between two firms of architects (Joseph Esherick is responsible for the design of another section) and Lawrence Halprin, the landscape architect. The client, Oceanic Properties, Inc., was also represented by an architect, Alfred Boeke, the firm's vice-president and planning director, who had formerly been on the faculty of the University of Southern California.

In the first section of the development, designed by Moore and his associates, individual condominium units have been assembled (not merely clustered or grouped) to form a single building, bold enough in its overall shape to command the coastline, yet composed diversely enough in its parts, internal and external, to satisfy the genuine need for individual expression and identification (*Figs. 75–76*). Lyndon writes, "Almost immediately we recognized the . . . need for a space that would be *either* outside or in; outside the boundaries of the main space, yet protected from the wind and open to the view and sun. Such an intermediate space, between the outside and an inner volume, occurs often in the work of Lou Kahn and has been an important feature of several of our recent buildings. For Sea Ranch we envisaged, at the outset, a quite closed and distinct main space with a controlled supplementary volume in which one could sit on the edge of the windy and spectacular coast. With this in mind we turned our attention to setting a group of such units into the land." These units are grouped together around a courtyard. The use of the shed roofs, because of the configuration of the site, gives a variety of vertical dimensions to the identically sized dwelling units. "The planes, rather than building to a closed geometrical figure, intersect each other to produce projecting tower units and retain an episodic complexity."[44]

The Swim Club at Sea Ranch extends the concept of the original condominium to a building of some civic importance to the community (*Fig. 77*). Recognizing the demands of the climate, the simple wood structure is backed into the side of a miniature valley to form the north wall of a sheltered courtyard opening to the sun. A traditional gable shape, extended into the slope of the hill, is split down its middle to suggest a wall though projecting elements and bracing members recall the completed shape.

Because the project suffered from drastic budget cuts—the pool and lockers shrank, the antigrotto (a projected swimming hole) was eliminated—Moore, acting on Boeke's suggestion, asked Barbara Stauffacher, a graphic designer, to try and save the day. Mrs. Stauffacher's exuberant essay in what has come to be called "supergraphics" includes arrows, stripes, and a host of other signs and devices that suggest direction and emphasize the complicated spatial and structural relationships of the building (*Fig. 78*). "It's a bit like

75. *Charles W. Moore, Donlyn Lyndon, William Turnbull, Richard Whitaker: Sea Ranch residential resort, north of San Francisco, California, 1965. View from the Pacific Ocean.*

76. *The architect's apartment at Sea Ranch. Interior.*

77. *Charles W. Moore, Donlyn Lyndon, William Turnbull, Richard Whitaker: Sea Ranch Swim Club, 1966. View from swimming pool.*

78. *Barbara Stauffacher, graphics: Sea Ranch Swim Club. Interior view of lockers.*

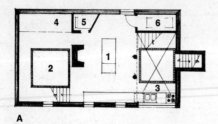

A Basement Floor
1. Dining Room
2. Study (open to above)
3. Kitchen
4. Reference Board
5. Furnace
6. Oil Tank

A

B First Floor
1. Living Room
2. Entry
3. Staircase

C Second Floor
1. Master Bedroom
2. Guest Bedroom
3. Bathroom
4. Roof
5. Skylight

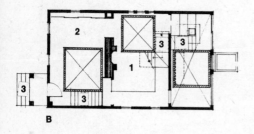

B

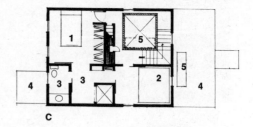

C

79. *The architect's house in New Haven, Connecticut, 1966. Plans.*

80. *The architect's house in New Haven. Exterior.*

a three-dimensional internal sculpture house that you can walk into," Mrs. Stauffacher has stated, "and it's a bit of a shocker: the exterior is all wood and shingles. The inside is a kinesthetic world of shapes and color."[45]

Moore's own house in New Haven, designed since his arrival at Yale, is a fascinating development beyond the unit design at the Sea Ranch. Inside an early-nineteenth-century house, Moore has inserted three vertical tubes of space to carry light into the interior from above and to transform the boxlike plan of the house into a constantly shifting composition of separate but interdependent spaces (*Figs. 79–81*). Ghastly colors, such as "eye-ease" green, are used in a deliberate way to shock but not necessarily exhaust the eye. Shapes, especially in the cutouts which extend walls into handrails and parapets, are implied across space and extended beyond the volume of the house itself. Moore states, "I wanted these graphics to seem like part of an even bigger world. It is a latter-day manifestation of a Piranesi complex. The 18th Century got its kicks by drawing the people too small, and I thought I could get mine by making the graphics twice too big. These are like pieces of great wheels rolling around and grinding over you."[46]

81. *The architect's house in New Haven. Interior.*

Under Moore, the direction of Yale's policies in architecture have swung from an emphasis on shape elaboration (as was the case under his predecessor, Paul Rudolph) toward a concern for the usefulness of architecture in relation to the problems of life in our less-advantaged areas, in our cities, and in our backwater locales.

Moore's interest in architectural education, like that of his former associate, Donlyn Lyndon, is a serious one that goes beyond the all too prevalent tendency of architects, young architects especially, to accept teaching positions for financial security or as a means of imposing their own particular view of the world on students. In a recent article, Moore has sketched "a short and highly prejudiced recent history of architecture, to describe a land eroded with pitfalls in a search for the developable area that remains."[47]

In this statement, Moore forges a curriculum that, it is hoped, reflects the concern of young architects with real problems leading to an actual solution, that is, a building. The first product of this approach is a community center for the citizens of New Zion, Kentucky, a rural

82. *Architecture students at Yale University: New Zion Community Center, New Zion, Appalachia, Kentucky, 1967. Sections and plans.*

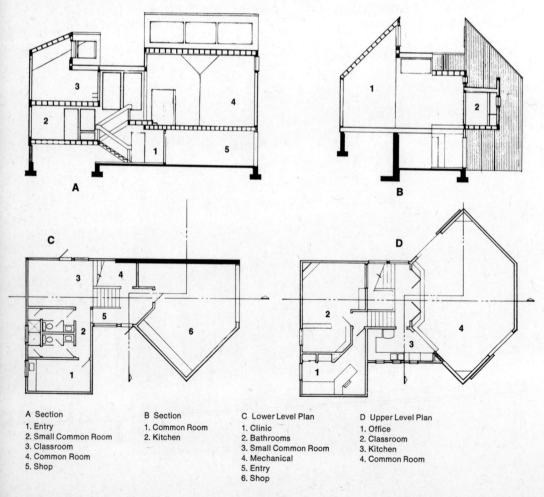

A Section	B Section	C Lower Level Plan	D Upper Level Plan
1. Entry	1. Common Room	1. Clinic	1. Office
2. Small Common Room	2. Kitchen	2. Bathrooms	2. Classroom
3. Classroom		3. Small Common Room	3. Kitchen
4. Common Room		4. Mechanical	4. Common Room
5. Shop		5. Entry	
		6. Shop	

community in Appalachia. Students worked with the residents of New Zion while, simultaneously (for this was part of the regular school program and not a casual "summer project"), participating in basic design studies in New Haven which would develop means for translating New Zion's needs into a building (*Figs. 82–83*). As to the community center itself, completed in spring, 1967, Moore states, "As an object it is a success...thanks to the scale of its big room and of its openings, it does not look like a house, yet is, because of its construction and materials, sympathetic to the simple buildings of the scattered rural community. It is apparently a place where it is fun to be, where a basket ball can be bounced at the same time that ladies are sewing without this seeming unpleasant for anyone. Because it was simple, because it was built by people that the members of the community liked and enjoyed having among themselves, because it used some of the efforts of the members of the community itself, it is apparently regarded not as an alien intrusion or as something some Martians from Yale left behind, but as a useful facility which is a part of New Zion."[48]

83. *New Zion Community Center (center). General view.*

ARCHITECTURE AND THE CITY

Urban Renewal

ORTHODOX modern architecture renounces idiosyncratic buildings in favor of abstract types, and for this reason the urbanistic capabilities of the International Style are limited. Together with its puristic formal preferences, this search for universal "types," as Le Corbusier described them, is responsible for the failure of orthodox modern architects and planners to go beyond individual monuments toward a true urbanism in which new and old buildings exist in mutually dependent relationships. A recognition of the incomplete and impure form of the modern city, in effect a recognition of an evolving hierarchy of urban values, distinguishes the inclusive from the exclusive approach to city design. Architects and planners alike, as Jane Jacobs, the urban critic and an early spokesman for the inclusive approach, points out, have been for so long concerned "about how cities *ought* to work and what *ought* to be good for people and businesses in them . . . . that when contradictory reality intrudes, threatening to shatter their dearly won learning, they must shrug reality aside."[49]

Mrs. Jacobs is alarmingly accurate when she writes that "The pseudo-science of city planning and its companion, the art of city design, have not yet broken with the specious comfort of wishes, familiar superstitions, oversimplifications, and symbols, and have not yet embarked upon the adventure of probing the real world."[50]

The generally accepted view of urban redevelopment, an outgrowth of Le Corbusier's Voisin Plan for rebuilding Paris, holds that to rebuild the city, each section of the city must in turn be destroyed. This "cataclysmic" view of city design, as Vincent Scully describes it, cannot and does not work.[51] Its assumption that all that has gone before is no longer relevant because it is old is morally as well as economically indefensible. We cannot sustain that permanent revolution which orthodox modern architecture has as its basis without destroying our cities and the heritage of our past. Some of the reasons why this attitude toward the renewal process still prevails, despite its obvious limitations, have to do with the limited vision of the men in charge of urban redevelopment, men who rely on accepted images and who, never having been trained to act as clients and having been given vast amounts of capital to dispose of, must justify their power with spectacular presentations and enormous projects rather than with the less dramatic adjustments which are often all that is needed to redirect the growth of a community. The natural process of urban renewal is one of little bits and pieces as much as it is one of giant strides.

Urban renewal was exploited in the 1950's and early 1960's as a way to bolster sagging urban economies. It substituted the bulldozer for planning and became, as Scully points out, "a device to turn the old New Deal around in order to use the taxes of the poor to subsidize their own removal for the benefit of real estate men, bankers, suburbanites and center city retailers."[52] The results can be seen most clearly in the efforts of Robert Moses, New York's city rebuilder, whose bulldozer, had it been left unchecked, would have destroyed virtually the entire West Side of Manhattan from 59th to 110th Streets. The Lincoln Center Urban Renewal Area can be regarded as Moses' principal achievement in city rebuilding: two massive projects in search of a neighborhood, one for culture (Lincoln Center for the Performing Arts), the other for living (Lincoln Towers; *Fig. 84*).

The West Side Urban Renewal Area in New York City was conceived in 1958 by Samuel Ratensky as an answer to Moses' methods (*Fig. 85*).[53] It was the first renewal project to eschew the cataclysmic approach. It substituted extensive rehabilitation of the decrepit but once elegant brownstones on the side streets leading west from Central Park, concentrating new apartment construction along Columbus Avenue, where an elevated railroad structure, torn down in 1916, had spawned tenements of the worst sort. The streets were turned back to pedestrians, in part at least, through the use of "neckdowns"—occasional sidewalk widenings on the side streets—used to locate benches and plantings and along the avenues for double rows of trees and outdoor cafes. The success of the West Side Urban Renewal Area can be measured, in that it is virtually indistinguishable from the surrounding area in the fundamental questions of buildings, mass, and siting. The community mix, racial and economic, is amazingly broad through the use of leased public housing in middle income cooperatives and other legal controls. It is not, like Lincoln Towers, a superblocked enclave of repeated buildings with a homogeneous economic and class tenancy. Lincoln Center and the West Side Urban Renewal Area represent polar extremes of the urban renewal process and of the exclusivist and inclusivist approaches to rebuilding cities.

Washington, D.C.'s Southwest Renewal Area is a kind of casebook of approaches to city development within an exclusivist framework. Given the Moses-like approach—rejecting as it does virtually all that is in a given place in favor of a policy of massive clearance and fresh starts—the Southwest, questionable sociology aside, is a relative success from the point of view of design. In this project, 552 acres of the southwest quadrant of the city, just beyond the governmental core at Capitol Hill, were leveled with the exception of a few historic houses, some community buildings, and an existing low-rent public housing project.

84. *Lincoln Center Urban Renewal Area, upper West Side, New York, N.Y. Air view taken in 1966 showing Lincoln Center for the Performing Arts (center), 1962–68, and Lincoln Towers Apartments (upper right), 1958–66.*

85. *West Side Urban Renewal Area, upper West Side, New York, N.Y., 1960– . View of interior courtyard surrounded by new public and middle-income housing as well as rehabilitated brownstones. Courtyard design by M. Paul Friedberg & Associates.*

The Southwest is as much an exercise in urban removal as in urban renewal: the preexisting population densities are reduced by about one quarter; few, if any, of the people who lived there before can afford to move back since redevelopment. As a substitute for an overall plan, the supervising agency offered piecemeal redevelopment parcels—superblocks that are unrelated to each other and to Washington's complicated grid pattern. At the core, there is a suburban-style shopping center and apartments designed by I. M. Pei afloat in a sea of cars, and remote from the existing as well as the planned public facilities (*Figs. 86–87*). Around it are individual projects (development parcels), each planned independently from the others so that the possibilities for coherent neighborhood development are minimized. Not only do the shapes of the various buildings differ but also the underlying attitude toward the amenities of urban life. Planning responsibility falls to each sponsor's architect with almost no overall controls.

At the level of individual project design, a recognition of the need for density (tall buildings) and the nostalgia for town life (low buildings, narrow streets, and private courtyards) results in what Percy Johnson-Marshall, an English writer on city design, describes as "a Tweedledum-Tweedledee battle taking place between the folksy, the whimsy—and the brutal."[54] This is most painfully apparent in the section designed by Charles M. Goodman, an architect otherwise known for excellent, modest house designs, where a black-and-silver apartment slab separates the poor, living in a preexisting public housing project, from the middle rich, living in the townhouse complex of his River Park development. In contrast to these are I. M. Pei's twin slabs which reflect in their siting an ordered acceptance of redevelopment at a new and big scale that is related to the street system and to the larger needs of the community.

The various parcels designed by Keyes, Lethbridge and Condon, admirable for their sophisticated design, are less satisfying by ordinary standards of use (*Fig. 88*). The pinwheel plan of slabs and townhouses is very disorienting; this confusion is heightened by the placement of townhouse entrances along the interior courts so that the normal order of streetscape is reversed. In addition, the raising up of the slabs on boldly shaped pilotis and the general brutalism of the overall design overwhelm the open spaces and make them uncomfortable to be in.

The parcels designed by Chloethiel Woodard Smith offer marked contrasts to the formal rectitude of the Pei and Keyes designs. Mrs. Smith is an architect who understands to a greater measure than most the role of familiar forms in the architecture of towns. In her work in the Southwest, and in subsequent projects such as La Clede Town, in St. Louis, with its corner "pubs" and neighborhood shops, she has succeeded, as few housing architects have, in injecting into new projects what Wolf Von Eckardt describes as "a sense of place."

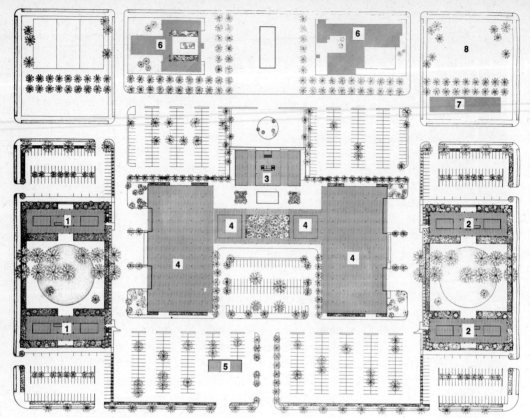

1. Town Center Plaza West
2. Town Center Plaza East
3. Town Center Office Building
4. Town Center Shopping
5. Service Station
6. Church
7. Library
8. Park

86. *I. M. Pei & Partners: Town Center Apartments, Southwest Urban Renewal Area, Washington, D. C., 1962. Site plan.*

87. *Town Center Development. General view.*

88. *Keyes, Lethbridge & Condon: Tiber Island, Southwest Urban Renewal Area, Washington, D.C., 1965. General view.*

89. *Chloethial Woodard Smith and Associated Architects: Capital Park, Southwest Urban Renewal Area, Washington, D.C., 1961. Air view.*

The evolution of Mrs. Smith's architecture, wildly eclectic and often overly cute, but always appropriately scaled and carefully considered from the viewpoint of urban design, can be traced in her work in the Southwest. In her first project there, Capitol Park Apartments, an ordinary parti of townhouse rows and tall slabs is transformed into a believable and inhabitable place, where the use of pergolas and fences allow cars to be seen but not to dominate, where streets give onto front doors and rear doors give onto gardens, where paint and small details suggest individuality within a basically repetitious organization and where open space is modulated to fulfill various functional and psychological needs (*Fig. 89*).

Harbour Square, a more recent design of Mrs. Smith's for the Southwest, takes these same techniques and intensifies them to provide for a denser development nearer to the center of the redevelopment area. Through the use of split levels and decks, parking is totally enclosed but not in a basement (and is thereby related to grade and to the life of the community), while the landscaped pedestrian spaces are so adroitly handled that, though many are above the level of the street, they do not appear divorced from its life (*Figs. 90–91*). Here, again, the parti is an obvious one though highly unorthodox in orthodox modern architecture: a street faces buildings surrounding a courtyard which gives onto another, the fourth side of which is left open to take advantage of a river view.

If the Southwest can be seen as a representative example of an exclusivist approach to urban redevelopment, the work of Carlin-Millard in New Haven can be seen as an inclusivist architectural response to an overly exclusivist planning framework. Much has been written about the achievements of New Haven's redevelopment program (which is a continuing one, begun in the early 1950's) and now, after the riots there in August 1967, about its failures.[55] A few things are clear; a good deal of what has been built there has been mediocre and, in the kinds of ways that are destructive to the fabric of the city and the lives of its citizens. Buildings surrounded by parking lots, un-mixed land uses so that areas function by the clock and can never become neighborhoods characterize New Haven's more showy efforts in its downtown. Some glamorous buildings have been built to attract suburbanites to the city but very little has been built for the people who were already there. As the saying goes in New Haven: "The poor? They now live in Bridgeport!" In trying to make itself over in terms of a dream—suburban and white—that should have died at least twenty years ago, New Haven has produced very little of lasting value. An exception to this, is the work that Earl P. Carlin, together with his design associate Peter Millard, has been able to produce: a handful of buildings which offer working images—believable on a day-to-day basis (not the Sunday-best of culture centers nor the gloss glamour of junior-department-store architecture and other commercial packages)—of what redevelopment could be like if architects and laymen

90. *Chloethial Woodard Smith and Associated Architects: Harbour Square, Southwest Urban Renewal Area, Washington, D.C., 1966. Model.*

91. *Harbour Square townhouses including restored "Wheat Row," c. 1795.*

both would accept once again that, as Millard has written, "the art of architecture is not a basic cause of culture but rather an expression of it; the role of the architect is not to affirm and establish his personal whim but rather to seek out and explore various ways to express the values of his culture."[56]

Carlin-Millard's work for the New Haven redevelopment agency has been in the residential neighborhoods outside the central business district. Here New Haven wisely pursued a limited policy of renewal, emphasizing conservation of sound older buildings and the introduction of new construction—often of a civic nature—at key locations. Carlin-Millard's Central Fire Station is just such a structure, intended to transcend functional requirements and to provide a symbolic gateway to the Wooster Square neighborhood (*Fig. 92*). This is achieved on a difficult and irregular site through an unorthodox organization of structure, and a skillful recall of billboard form that prefigures Robert Venturi's proposal for a "bill-ding-board" at the Football Hall of Fame (*see Figs. 50–51*). The Central Fire House adjoins a railroad right-of-way and though it marks the entrance to a residential area is not actually in it.

92. *Earl P. Carlin and Peter Millard: Central Fire Station, New Haven, Connecticut, 1959–62. General view.*

In the Whitney Avenue Fire Station, Carlin-Millard demonstrated that a similar, if somewhat reduced program, could be inserted into a quiet residential area and that a working facility could be produced that was compatible in scale with the neighborhood without need of camouflage (*Fig. 93*). To the claims that the building is "clapboard-Gothic" Millard writes, "That's all right. I had been wondering for a long time whether we could put a building together in a way that would not only have the capacity to be interpreted in a familiar way, but also in an unfamiliar way. I thought about how we could organize a building that would be clearly whatever it needed to be within itself and not be inappropriate to what was already there before. ...Our intention was to organize the building in such a way that it would embody these characteristics in terms of its being a self-contained building as well as a member of a community."[57]

Columbus Mall Houses illustrates that the inclusive approach can extend to complexes of buildings on sites cleared in typical renewal-removal fashion within existing neighborhoods (*Fig. 94*).

93. *Earl P. Carlin and Peter Millard: Whitney Avenue Fire Station, New Haven, Connecticut, 1964. General view.*

94. *Earl P. Carlin and Peter Millard: Columbus Mall Houses, Wooster Square Urban Renewal Area, New Haven, Connecticut, 1965. General view.*

Despite the redevelopment agency's insistence that the architects incorporate suburban amenities into the project (though it is only five blocks from City Hall and adjacent to Wooster Square, New Haven's most urbane open space), a dogged acceptance of the economic limitations of the program and a real sense of responsibility to the place and to the kinds of people who use it has resulted in a scheme that, if not exactly dazzling in form, is at least alive to the moment and the means available, using standardized materials of seemingly little aesthetic promise and combining them in fresh ways that are relevant to the requirements of the program and the qualities of the place.

A truly inclusive approach to renewal is now being pursued in New York City, where a program of vest-pocket public and middle-income housing, now being designed under the supervision of the Housing and Development Administration and the New York City Housing Authority, is, in its recognition of community preferences for design sympathetic to the shapes of preexisting buildings, making the beginning steps toward a means of rebuilding cities without destroying communities (*Fig. 95*). For the first time since the early 1940's, low-rise public housing is being built in New York—and not free standing on huge superblocks but as infill along streets, not oriented in accord with some ideal sun-and-exposure chart, but in accord with the neighborhood development pattern and with the wishes of the people who live there.[58]

95. *The City of New York Housing and Development Administration, Office of Planning, Design and Research: Model Cities schematic design study 221 D 3, Vest Pocket Housing, 1968. Isometric view.*

The vest-pocket housing program in New York is the most extensive program of its kind thus far undertaken. It is not a substitute for long-range planning, nor does it discount the need for massive slum clearance in some areas; it is, instead, an urban solution to a traditional urban problem: the gradual replacement of worn out parts. It is an affirmation that once again it is possible for architects to contribute to the agglutinative process of urban growth and to relate wholly modern buildings to those of the past. It is symbolic of an attitude toward cities that is evolutionary and not revolutionary.

Formal Preoccupations and Prejudices

Looking at the broadest questions of urban form and at the nature of American cities as they *are*, it becomes apparent that, as Charles W. Moore has written, "architects, and especially architecture students, continue to fly in the face of all the available facts, with the breathless announcement that the only problem worth their consideration is the super-high-density pedestrian urban core of the sort which continues to exist in New York, Calcutta, Provincetown, Carmel, and a diminishing list of other places. . . ."[59] Just as Mayor John V. Lindsay has made it clear that New York City's problems are not merely bigger editions of those in other cities but also very different, so it must be emphasized that despite the homogenizing effects of mass communication, the scale and quality of urban life varies from place to place and that, in fact, a new kind of urban life is already with us—one which was anticipated at least thirty years ago by Frank Lloyd Wright who, building upon the ideas of Le Corbusier, imagined a diffuse city at the scale of the automobile. Los Angeles is such a city as are the vast suburbs on Long Island, in the Maryland countryside between Baltimore and Washington, D.C., in the plains west of Chicago, around the San Francisco Bay and elsewhere, everywhere. And, contrary to what some professionals would have us believe, the people who live in this new, unhierarchical (uniform scale) landscape with linear centers (commercial strip developments) appear to be happy. The fact that they live the way they do, and that significant numbers elect to do so every year, is a continuing demonstration that, as Moore puts it, "you can do almost anything you need to do in a city almost anywhere."[60]

The necessary urbanism which we think we lack can only come about if architects and clients recognize that a city is more than a lot of idiosyncratic buildings fighting for aesthetic survival and that urban design and urban planning are one and the same, having to do with the highly divergent relationships between hierarchy and function which are to be found from place to place in America at this time.

The extent to which orthodox modern architecture has blinded us to traditional city architecture as an expression of life styles at a given moment can be measured in the endless intimations of the Piazza San Marco surrounded by free-standing buildings with parking lots behind. As Robert Venturi points out, the "piazza compulsion" is in fact " 'un-American.' Americans feel uncomfortable sitting in a square. They should be working at the office or home with the family looking at television or perhaps at a bowling alley. Chores around the house or the weekend drive replace the passeggiata. . . . We are in the habit of calling open space precious in the city. It is not. Except in Manhattan perhaps, our cities have too much open space in the ubiquitous parking lots, in the not-so-temporary deserts created by urban renewal and in the amorphous suburbs around."[61]

This "piazza compulsion" relates to an even more destructive urge, the urge to suburbanize not only the open country but the developed city as well. As Wolf Von Eckardt points out, "The freeways, with their exorbitant space demands, the setbacks that disrupt the harmony of the street, the whole, almost obsessive emphasis on 'open space' within the city, further blur the distinction between the suburbs and downtown. The idea is that cities are too crowded and must be opened up. Our recent architecture and urban design are opening up to excess. The result is that . . . this fashion ab-

96. *Charles DuBose, coordinating architect, Sasaki, Dawson, DeMay Associates, urban designers: Constitution Plaza, Hartford, Connecticut, 1964. General view looking north.*

stracts the city. It deliberately and somewhat rebelliously replaces familiar images with willful, intuitively designed, though highly rationalized, forms. They create a jumble of high and low. Buildings jut out or stay back and are placed at odd angles."[62]

Typical of this mistaken desire to open up the dense core of cities is Constitution Plaza, Hartford, where a kind of cloud-cuckoo land of irrelevent plazas and levels two floors above the street and accessible only by steep flights of stairs, divorced from the life of the city and without sufficient life to sustain itself, has been produced, removing rather than renewing the life of the place. (*Fig. 96*).[63] In San Francisco, by contrast, after one major and thoroughly delightful open space was created facing the Bay at Ghirardelli Square, the architects of the adjacent Cannery, a sophisticated retailing facility *did not* try to repeat the initial success but instead to complement it. The Cannery is antispatial in conception with stairs, elevators, and passageways that respect movement from one place to another rather than suggest the lingering of a plaza (*Figs. 97–98*).

Architects have offered "plazas" as a substitute for any real

97. *Lawrence Halprin & Associates, urban design, Bernardi and Emmons, architects: Ghirardelli Square, San Francisco, California, 1965. View from San Francisco Bay.*

thinking about buildings and open space and, by extension, cities themselves. In focusing their urbanistic concerns on the plaza as the principal ornament of city design, they have abrogated to the highway engineers the right to design a good deal of America's open space. Charles W. Moore suggests that architects might seek to "develop a vocabulary of forms responsive to the marvelously complex and varied functions of our society, instead of continuing to impose vague generalizations with which we presently add to the grayness of the suburban sea. Then, we might start sorting out for our special attention those things for which the public has to pay, from which might derive the public life. . . ." Moore, in contrast to Wolf Von Eckardt, thinks that "The freeways could be the real monuments of the future, the places set aside for special celebration by people able to experience space and light and motion and relationships to other people and things at a speed that so far only this century has allowed. Here are structures big enough and strong enough, once they are regarded as part of the city, to reexcite the public imagination about the city. This is no shame to be covered by suburban bushes or quarantined behind cyclone fences. It is the marker for a place set in motion, transforming itself to another place."[64] Moore's remarks may be prophetic but are as yet unrealized (except in a number of studies about the design of roads and their physical as well as social impact, now being financed by the federal government and others, which may alter all our thinking about them).

The compulsion to build towers is equal in its destructive capabilities to the urge to build plazas. Locked into modern planning theory since Le Corbusier's Voisin Plan, it has been regarded as axiomatic that high density can only be provided in an environmentally satisfactory manner through the use of towers. A few recent projects suggest that it is possible to build at high densities without losing the sense of enclosure and spatial definition that only buildings acting as walls rather than as point markers (towers) can provide. A good example of high-density urban housing, without the use of towers can be seen in Sert, Jackson and Gourley's Francis Greenwood Peabody Terrace Apartments for married students at Harvard University (*Fig. 99*). Here, separated slabs of varying heights (and interconnected by bridges) define generously proportioned courtyards, which provide a necessary sense of privacy and enclosure for the residents without sacrificing the definition of the streets at the periphery.

Riverbend, along the Harlem River in Manhattan, by Davis, Brody and Associates, is a similar scheme, and even more boldly scaled (*Figs. 100–101*). More closely integrated with the development pattern of the neighborhood than Peabody Terrace, Riverbend goes beyond Peabody in the arrangement of the apartments, with pedestrian "streets in the sky" providing access to duplex apartments opening off front yards, and in its evocation of the individual

98. *Joseph Esherick and Associates: The Cannery, San Francisco, California, 1968. View of courtyard.*

99. *Sert, Jackson and Gourley: Francis Greenwood Peabody Terrace, married student housing, Harvard University, Cambridge, Massachusetts, 1964. General view.*

100. *Davis, Brody and Associates: Riverbend Houses, Harlem River Drive and 138th Street, New York, N.Y., 1968. General view.*

101. *Riverbend Houses. Section perspective, showing typical duplexes with "front porch" and "street in the sky."*

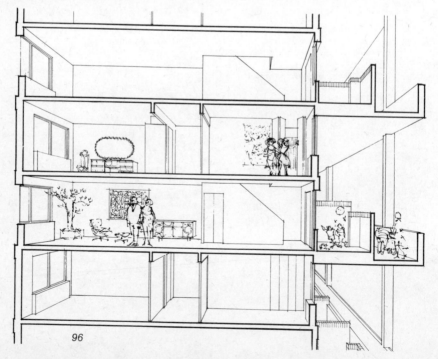

dwelling unit within a framework for mass housing. A more recent proposal by this firm, East Midtown Apartments in the Bellevue South Urban Renewal Area of New York City, and now under construction, emphasizes the continuity between the high and low units through the use of a complex and deliberately blurred geometry of wall surfaces which combine tower and low space—separate buildings blend into one continuous structure (*Fig. 102*). East Midtown Plaza is a strong piece of urban design because it does many things at once: the fronts and backs of towers and low buildings define streets, create interior spaces, and insure that each space will have its own character, though related to that of the project and that of the town. As Lawrence Halprin, the landscape architect, has written, East Midtown Plaza "exhibits as sensitive a response to siting and open space design as we have seen at work in the city. A real attempt has been made to maintain the urban grain, integrate the buildings with an existing church, and develop a sequence of interior handsome squares and recreation spaces."[65]

The principal thrust of the inclusive approach to city rebuilding is preservationist in the broadest sense: it seeks to build for the life styles of people and not to alter them to suit some abstract sense of form. It also seeks to reinforce the qualities of urbanity that some of our cities already possess. For example, the urge to open up the grid in Manhattan has contributed to a general breakdown of the

102. *Davis, Brody and Associates: East Midtown Plaza, Bellevue South Urban Renewal Area, 23rd Street between First and Second Avenues, New York, N.Y., phase one to be completed c. 1971. Perspective drawing.*

essential character of the place. As a result of the zoning ordinance adopted in 1961, the old, urbanistically sound pattern of dense blocks of buildings gradually diminishing in size as they rise to slim, free-standing towers, "a graphic expression of metropolitan pressure," as the British architect James Stirling observes, (and a pattern capable of generating linked pedestrian arcades along streets and through blocks) has been replaced with a pattern of free-standing towers in mini-plazas which are unrelated to any overall plan for open space and are, in fact, for a good part of the year, merely drafty and dusty.[66] The gridiron plan of Manhattan Island, though frought with shortcomings, has at the very least fostered one of the few memorable urban environments of this century.

103. *Reinhard, Hofmeister, Morris, Corbett, Harmon and MacMurray, Hood and Fouilhoux: Rockefeller Center, 48th to 50th Street between Fifth and Sixth Avenues, New York, N.Y., 1931–40. Air view.*

Rockefeller Center, conceived in and largely built by 1932, remains the preeminent example of what urban design can achieve within the grid pattern of development, with linked underground concourses, and a major *defined* open space with a shop-lined mall leading to a skating rink and restaurants, all related to those passages and to the streets (*Fig. 103*). But in planning a westward expansion the architects for the Center, at this writing, are considering the abandonment of almost all the pioneering features of the original development in favor of a loose site plan of volumetrically unrelated towers and in so doing would fail to provide those amenities which made Rockefeller Center unique. It is not entirely their fault. The zoning ordinance encourages this; and its most recently completed irony is the new General Motors Building, which, bulk and facade design aside, is set back from Fifth Avenue to reveal a sunken plaza in front of Grand Army Plaza, formerly one of the loveliest spaces in Manhattan, while at the other end of the block Madison Avenue starves for open space (*Fig. 104*). The point is that open spaces in cities are needed but that, in most cases, they demand a kind of planning that extends beyond the limits of individual sites and commercialism—that kind of planning which is needed if zoning is to be a useful tool capable of insuring more in the way of urban amenities than just light and air. In New York the Planning Commission has assembled an Urban Design Group to advise it and thereby begin to make possible the administration of zoning as much a function of design as it is of economics and political pressure.[67]

In order to prevent another disaster such as that at the General Motors Building, the Urban Design Group is manipulating the open space bonus provision of the zoning ordinance and other special permit provisions to provide a series of linked open spaces connecting Chase Manhattan Plaza (Skidmore, Owings and Merrill, 1960) with the 110-story twin towers of the World Trade Center (Minoru Yamasaki and Emery Roth and Sons, to be completed in 1975) now under construction in the financial district; it is trying to extend the character of the original Rockefeller Center development into its western territories; it is also instrumental in creating around Times Square a special theater district so that redevelopment by the private sector will include theaters in new office buildings in the hope that this will enhance rather than destroy the vitality of the area as we now know it.

Reintegration and Renewal

A vast number of projects have already been built embodying the principles of the cataclysmic approach, eliminating entire neighborhoods and replacing them with evenly spaced towers and vast empty, open spaces. It is to these, the housing and renewal projects of the forties and fifties (such as the phalanx of low-income apartments along Manhattan's East River Drive, and Chicago's Lake Meadows development) that urban designers must turn their attention. These projects represent too much in the way of capital investment and social commitment to be replaced for another half century, if even that soon, yet they are a constant reminder of the poverty of spirit which has marked recent attempts at city rebuilding. It is clear that ways must be found to integrate—to include—such projects into the fabric of the preexisting city. This is very difficult because, as Lawrence Halprin writes in *New York, New York,* a report on "the quality, character, and meaning of open space in urban design," that "We have very little 'hard' information on how people *really* react to their environment. What we have had is novelistic-romantic or poetic, inferred rather than studied, hoped for rather than assured."[68] In a typical project in New York City, Penn Station South,

104. *Edward Durrell Stone and Emery Roth and Sons, associated architects: General Motors Building, Fifth Avenue between 58th and 59th Streets, New York, N.Y., 1968. Air view showing General Motors' sunken plaza in relation to Grand Army Plaza.*

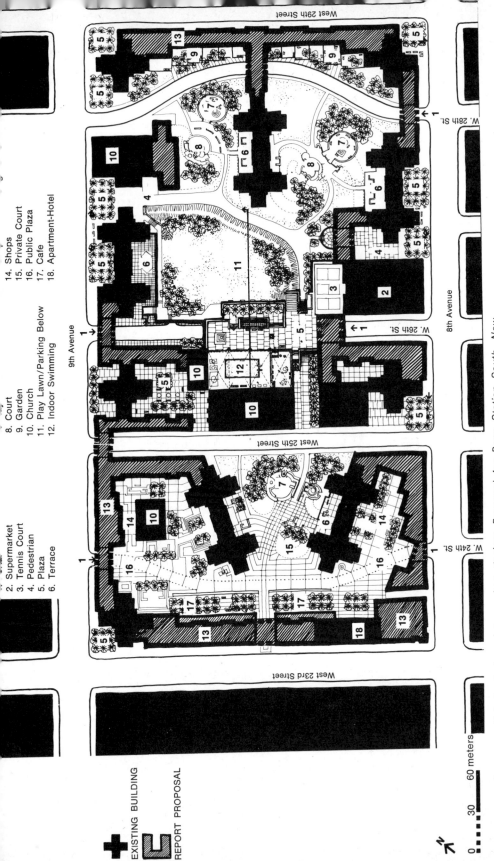

1. ~~Existing Building~~
2. Supermarket
3. Tennis Court
4. Pedestrian
5. Plaza
6. Terrace

8. Court
9. Garden
10. Church
11. Play Lawn/Parking Below
12. Indoor Swimming

14. Shops
15. Private Court
16. Public Plaza
17. Cafe
18. Apartment-Hotel

West 29th Street

W. 28th St.

8th Avenue

9th Avenue

W. 26th St.

West 25th Street

W. 24th St.

West 23rd Street

N

0 30 60 meters

EXISTING BUILDING

REPORT PROPOSAL

105. *Lawrence Halprin & Associates, urban design: Proposal for Penn Station South, New York, N.Y., published 1968. Site plan.*

in which the streetscape is fractured by towers rising from green lawns at no orthogonal relationship to the grid-iron plan of Manhattan, Halprin proposed that new six-story buildings link up the towers along the perimeter streets, forming courtyards inside which new recreational facilities would be placed (*Fig. 105*).

Though it is unlikely that Halprin's proposal for Penn Station South will be carried out, its influence is bound to be felt in other places such as the projected housing for the Seward Park neighborhood of Manhattan's Lower East Side (*Fig. 106*). In a similar, though far more aggravated situation, the notorious Pruitt-Igoe low-cost housing project in St. Louis, M. Paul Friedberg, the landscape architect, proposed to vary the social mix by introducing new middle-income housing and additional facilities while upgrading the physical environment (*Fig. 107*). Low-rise structures will be inserted in between the slabs to create more humanely scaled open spaces, to increase the density and make it possible to support the commercial and community facilities which can enrich life and help to knit the project into the fabric of the community by attracting people to it from the surrounding neighborhood. "If there is but one lesson to be learned from Pruitt-Igoe," Friedberg has stated, "it is that grouping together of large numbers of impoverished families exacerbates the social problems and diminishes every chance of achieving constructive social goals. We now know that to provide a safe, sound and sanitary dwelling unit is not enough."[69] Friedberg has gone far toward an

106. *William F. Pedersen, architect, Hanford Young, Fred Bookhardt, Jr., Robert Zimmerman, associates: Mitchell-Lama Project, Seward Park Extension, New York, N.Y., to be completed c. 1970. Perspective drawing.*

understanding of how today's children, with expectations vastly expanded (and jaded) by television and other communication forms, use open space.

At Jacob Riis Plaza, and countless smaller playgrounds and vest-pocket parks in Manhattan, Friedberg has developed a wholly new vocabulary of recreational furniture which, when properly understood, can be adapted by others (*Fig. 108*). Friedberg does not seek to adapt an abstract sculptural ideal to the function of play, as did Charles Forberg at the Cypress Hills Houses experimental playground sponsored by the Museum of Modern Art (*Fig. 109*). Friedberg works from an understanding of games and the motion of children and from these he constructs environments that are related to particular places: the very opposite of the standard and standardized play equipment (the endlessly dull see-saws) found in almost every children's park.

Not only must we take a fresh look at how new open spaces can be used but also at open space resources that go unnoticed in our cities. Primary among these are the streets themselves, which are usually too numerous and given over solely to cars. Friedberg, working in association with I. M. Pei, has demonstrated what can be done, within the existing framework of the grid-iron plan (which characterizes the older sections of most of our cities), to return streets to pedestrian use. Basing their designs on the neckdowns

107. *M. Paul Friedberg & Associates, landscape architects: Proposal for Pruit-Igoe, St. Louis, Missouri, project, 1967.*

108. *Pomerance and Breines, architects, M. Paul Friedberg & Associates, landscape architects: Jacob Riis Plaza, Avenue D, between 6th and 7th Streets, New York, N.Y., 1966. General view.*

first devised for the West Side Urban Renewal project, already mentioned, two streets are now closed and made into parks, scaled to the needs of the immediate community and providing each block with a usable focus (*Fig. 110*).

The New City?

Carried to its logical extreme, the exclusivist attitude calls for a wholly new and technological approach to city design. Some architects, excited by the great new technological developments at our disposal, seem to seek solutions that are sweeping in scope and bold in gesture. They have been tempted to imagine new cities at vast scale to replace what we now have, offering instead ideal solutions that rely on systems and technology still in experimental stages, and owe little to any hard analysis about how people want to live. By their very scope and scale of projected magnitude, these "megastructures" very often demand destruction of whole sections of towns which for economic and more importantly social reasons are questionable. They are difficult to imagine as places to live in, not so much because they are big, but because they appear rigid and incapable of adapting to the quirks of personal preference. Efforts to solve urban problems through technological innovation may be an attempt to camouflage the impatience which many architects feel

109. *Charles Forberg & Associates: Playground at Cypress Hills Houses, Brooklyn, New York, 1967. General view.*

110. *I. M. Pei & Partners, M. Paul Friedberg & Associates, landscape architects: Bedford-Stuyvesant superblock project and open space development demonstration in cooperation with The City of New York, Brooklyn, New York, under construction. Above, view of St. Marks Avenue prior to construction; below, perspective drawing of projected superblock.*

toward the processes and the complications of community relations which go hand in hand with the new, inclusive approach to city redevelopment.

Typical of these visionary cities, and of the kind of impatience with real problems that some architects of the exclusive school possess, is Stanley Tigerman's "Instant City" which, by its name and by its form suggest its limitations (*Fig. 111*). A variety of other proposals, in their emphasis on multidimensional organization, prefigure environments that seem unrelated to what is known (no matter how romanticized) about cities as places and about how people use cities. Such proposals as John M. Johansen's "Leapfrog City," though clothed in the formal vocabulary of the sixties, do not in fact, go beyond the intentions of Le Corbusier in the 1920's, replacing rather than rebuilding the city, and, ultimately, leaving all the disorder intact at the ground level (*Fig. 112*).

In the same way, the proposal for a community center perched atop an enormous tower set between rows of dense tenements, though dramatic, is not related to the little we know from experience with community buildings in recent decades and the writings of Edward Hall and Jane Jacobs, among too few others, about how people live in communities; it is remote and removed from the activities of daily life (*Fig. 113*). To the extent that proposals for development at a new scale relate to an attitude that excludes, to the extent that they aim to tidy up cities and organize them, they

111. *Stanley Tigerman: "Instant City," project, 1966. Model.*

can be said to be more important as comments upon the problems that exist rather than their solution. To the extent that they substitute some ideal of life for the messy facts of life as it is lived, they are unreal and, as importantly, unrealistic.

The technological approach to new cities does not so much deal with cities as substitute for them. Similarly, another method of approaching city problems, one that also excludes, and one that is as old as cities themselves, is that of fresh starts in pleasant rural surroundings: the suburb or garden city. Reston is such a place and its failures as well as its successes have much to say about the lip service so many Americans give to fighting the battle of the cities in the cities.

Reston is no more a solution to the problems of cities—merely removing itself from them—than the English Garden Cities of fifty years ago. Some of its architecture is handsome (*Fig. 114*), but its fate at the hands of the Gulf Oil Company is less a comment on the savagery of corporations than it is on the hopeless naiveté of the

112. *John M. Johansen: "Leapfrog City," project, 1966. Perspective sketch showing redevelopment of Park Avenue, New York, N.Y., looking south toward Pan Am building.*

113. *Hardy Holzman Pfeiffer Associates: Community Center as a Straddle Structure Brooklyn, New York, project, 1968. Composite view showing relationship of structure to Fort Greene neighborhood.*

original developer's approach. It is an attempt to recreate the physical characteristics of old cities rather than their ordering principles.

The plan for Reston is, in effect, not a plan but a diagram linked by roadways and dependent for its success on the merits of the work of individual architects (*Fig. 115*). It represents an exclusive approach but not a technologically determined one. Reston is a romantic notion of preindustrial village life and it derives its principal appeal from a skillful camouflaging of the complexities of economics and life at the fringe of a large city.

Reston is like Disneyland, which, as Charles W. Moore describes it, is not "some sort of physical extension of Mickey Mouse" but an important statement struggling to replace those elements to the public realm which have disappeared as the "floating world" of endless suburbs has enlarged itself. The difference between Disneyland and Reston (and other suburban "new towns") is that the daily life Reston imagines for us is removed from the life we really lead, while Disneyland is a place for holiday and one that, as Moore observes, "recreates all the chances to respond to a *public* environment . . . [allowing for] play-acting, both to be watched and to be participated

114. *William J Conklin and James S. Rossant: Reston. View of Lake Anne village center, 1964.*

115. *Julian H. Whittlesey, William J Conklin and James S. Rossant: Reston, Fairfax County, Virginia. Masterplan, 1962.*

A   Golf Course
B   Government Reserve
C   Health Complex
D   High School
E   Industrial Area
F   Intermediate School
G   Park
H   Post Graduate High School
J   Sports Park
K   Town Center
L   Outer Circumferential Highway
M   Railroad
N   Airport Access Highway

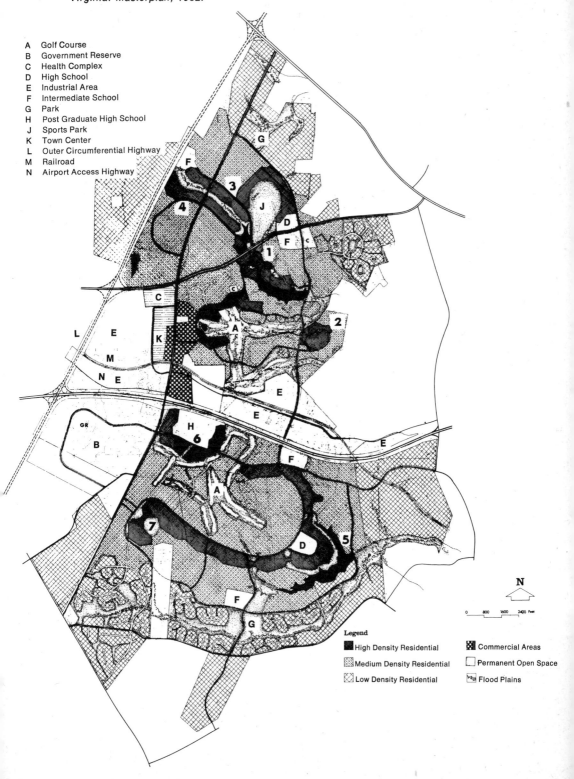

N

0   800   1600   2400 Feet

Legend

■ High Density Residential
▦ Medium Density Residential
▧ Low Density Residential

▦ Commercial Areas
□ Permanent Open Space
▨ Flood Plains

in, in a public sphere."[70] Disneyland does not offer up Venice or an Italian Hill Town as its principal urban attraction, but an image of a *Main Street*, of about 1910, with false-front architecture, trolleys and wagons, stores and people—all the trappings in fact of an ideal American town life. It is an American image and it works effortlessly because Americans instinctively know what to do there.

Columbia, another new town, between Washington, D.C., and Baltimore, promises to be more successful; its plan is more wholly comprehensive, its site more logical (between two metropolises) and its architectural goals more realistic: it is a rationalization of the typical suburban tract development, intensified in its population density and including areas for industry (*Fig. 116*). Its architecture is loosely controlled, but there is little of the conscious image-recall that characterizes Reston.

The proposal for the development of Sunset Mountain in California projects a single image for a whole new town (*Figs. 117–118*). Sunset Mountain is now unutilized though it is relatively close in to the various centers that make up Los Angeles. At the top of the mountain an urban center would provide parking, restaurants, shops,

116. *The Rouse Company: Columbia, Howard County, Maryland, to be completed 1980. Schematic plan.*

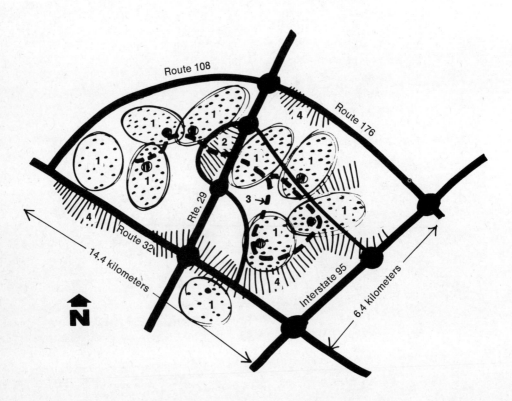

1. Village   2. Town Center   3. Bus Route   4. Commercial

and related community facilities within one building; along the face, 1,500 units of housing would be built in stages. Inclined elevators provide access to the terraced housing units and pneumatic tubes take care of the delivery of goods. Unlike "Instant City," Sunset Mountain grew out of a real site; like Columbia, it is a rational reorganization of the typical commercial situation—in this case a hillside tract development of the kind that is found all over California. As such, it seeks to reconstruct a current pattern of suburban development in accord with an older image of towns. Whether in so doing it "improves" this mode of development at the expense of its presumed advantages—private open space, individuality of dwelling units and possibilities for change, convenience in an automobile society—is not certain. What Sunset Mountain's scheme does suggest is that rational design can direct technology to problem-solving on an urban level without, on the one hand, excluding the familiar qualities of life and on the other, lapsing into that kind of picturesqueness which mars Paul Rudolph's plan for Stafford Harbor (*Fig. 119*). Based on a notion of architecture as an extension of landscape, and without the apparent systematic logic of Sunset Mountain, Stafford Harbor will have two kinds of buildings: housing along the ridges, and community facilities in the valleys, linked together and to the water by a road system. At the water's edge, as at Reston, a European townscape image complete with marina, paved plaza and campanile, is projected; the cars and the parking lots are neatly tucked behind.

Delightful though some of these new towns may be, the need for a new attitude toward the making of towns, one that is not inhibited by a fixed architectural image, is urgent. The lessons of sprawl and strip development must be recognized in our new towns; they cannot be wished away.

117. *Daniel, Mann, Johnson and Mendenhall, architects, C. Pelli, A. J. Lumsden, P. Jacobson, designers: Sunset Mountain Park Development, Los Angeles, California, project, 1965. Cross section.*

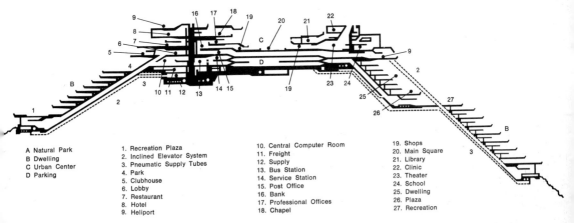

A Natural Park	1. Recreation Plaza	10. Central Computer Room	19. Shops
B Dwelling	2. Inclined Elevator System	11. Freight	20. Main Square
C Urban Center	3. Pneumatic Supply Tubes	12. Supply	21. Library
D Parking	4. Park	13. Bus Station	22. Clinic
	5. Clubhouse	14. Service Station	23. Theater
	6. Lobby	15. Post Office	24. School
	7. Restaurant	16. Bank	25. Dwelling
	8. Hotel	17. Professional Offices	26. Plaza
	9. Heliport	18. Chapel	27. Recreation

118. *Sunset Mountain Park Development. Model from above.*

119. *Paul Rudolph: Stafford Harbor, Virginia, 1966. View of harbor.*

AFTERWORD

THE best hope, the newest directions, it seems to me, lie with those who are now in the architecture schools and with what they are doing. True, some of the schools are still run like refined ateliers with masters and docile students designing, as in the hey-days of the École des Beaux-Arts, mythic places for mythic people. But in many schools, the clear air of real problems is now blowing through the drafting rooms. At Berkeley, at Rice, at Columbia, and at Yale, the vital questions of environmental design, design for life and not the reverse, are being tackled in a staggering variety of ways.

Columbia's architecture students, of course, have been the most sensationally outspoken. They were among the most articulate and committed in the student revolution during spring 1968 (and some of the basic issues—the gym and the physical growth of the university within the Morningside Heights community—were architectural ones in the profoundest sense). Whether the conduct of learning at Columbia is significantly better as a result of the shifting of values and goals is not yet clear, but two things have resulted from the increased commitment of students to the problems of their immediate environment that are of value: I. M. Pei has been retained by the Trustees to prepare the first coordinated development plan for the university since McKim, Mead & White produced theirs in 1897; and architecture students are going out into the community and trying to relate their learning experience to the problems, needs and desires of people. That there is danger in all of this, that it may take students too far from their craft, that it may encourage them to believe that sociology is architecture, is obvious. But at this time, a healthy dose of the "real world" is surely valuable.

At Yale, this fresh wind of creativity has lead students to investigate even less conventional areas of concern. Under Charles W. Moore's direction, students built a community center for a small town in Appalachia. Under Robert Venturi they went to Los Angeles and Las Vegas for two weeks and spent an entire semester "learning to love" the latter. The results of that cultivated courtship may be the most significant product to have come out of the new, non-ivory-tower approach to architectural education. Growing out of Venturi's belief that "a careful documentation and analysis of [Las Vegas'] physical form is as important to architects and urbanists today as were the studies of medieval Europe and ancient Rome and Greece to earlier generations," the students faced this place and phenomenon head-on and analyzed it in depth, using a variety of techniques including film and tape, producing a staggering amount of fresh graphical presentation. Thus, the new direction of architectural approach can be seen as nonsentimental and free of guilt (it is not only black life that American architects have ignored; it may well be all life). As the Yale students and Venturi put it, "The study of a place like the Las Vegas strip is a necessary prelude to discovering what the strip ought to be, and can be called applied design research —research undertaken by the architect as an aid to design."[71] This approach incorporates the "learning-by-doing" tradition of the hitherto conventional education (which is necessary if we are to produce architects who can function professionally) into a rich intellectual process in which research of a formal as well as an informational sort is conducted and results are sought (and often produced) which may be of value to others besides the individual who made them. This attitude, this anxiety over real problems, is as near to a new direction as anything in this book.

NOTES

1. Charles W. Moore, "Statement of the Jurors," *Progressive Architecture*, XLVIII, No. 1 (January 1967), 144.
2. Paul Rudolph, "For Perspecta," *Perspecta: The Yale Architectural Journal*, 7 (1961), p. 51.
3. Robert Venturi, *Complexity and Contradiction in Architecture* (New York, 1966), pp. 22, 23.
4. Philip Johnson, letter to Jason R. Nathan, Administrator, Housing and Development Administration, the City of New York, 12 March 1968.
5. Donlyn Lyndon, letter to Jason R. Nathan, Administrator, Housing and Development Administration, the City of New York, 15 March 1968.
6. Robert Venturi and Denise Scott Brown, "A Significance for A&P Parking lots or learning from Las Vegas," *Architectural Forum*, CXXVIII, No. 2 (March 1968), 37.
7. Louis I. Kahn, "Form and Design," reprinted in Vincent J. Scully, Jr., *Louis I. Kahn* (New York, 1962), pp. 114–121.
8. *Ibid.*
9. Romaldo Giurgola, "On Louis Kahn," *Zodiac*, XVII (1967), 119.
10. Statement by David Crane included in "Iconography and the Process of Architecture: The Jury's Conclusions," *Progressive Architecture*, XLVIII, No. 1 (January 1967), 168.
11. Louis I. Kahn, "Form and Design," reprinted in Scully, *Kahn*.
12. Romaldo Giurgola, "On Louis Kahn."
13. Vincent J. Scully, Jr., "Recent Works by Louis Kahn," *Zodiac*, XVII (1967), 58–117.
14. Romaldo Giurgola, "On Louis Kahn."
15. Vincent J. Scully, Jr. "Recent Works by Louis Kahn," p. 69.
16. Paul Rudolph, "The Six Determinants of Architectural Form," *Architectural Record*, CXX, No. 4 (October 1956), 183–186.
17. "New Directions of Paul Rudolph," *Perspecta*, 1 (1952), p. 21.
18. Paul Rudolph quoted by Robert A. M. Stern in "Secrets of Paul Rudolph (Paul Rudolph and His First Twenty-five Years)," *Kokusai Kentiku*, XXXII (April 1965), 55–58 (in Japanese).
19. Paul Rudolph, "The Six Determinants of Architectural Form."
20. Paul Rudolph quoted by Jonathan Barnett in "Speaking of Architecture," *Architectural Record*, CXXXI, No. 1 (January 1962), 74.
21. Paul Rudolph quoted in "House in the Sky—with terrace—under 221-D-3," *Architectural Record*, CXLIII, No. 7 (June 1968), 160.
22. Paul Rudolph, "Proposed Trailer Tower," *Perspecta*, 11 (1967), p. 191.
23. Paul Rudolph quoted in "The Mobile Home is the 20th Century Brick," *Architectural Record*, CXLIII, No. 4 (April 1968), 143.
24. Vincent J. Scully, Jr., *Modern Architecture* (New York, 1961), p. 118.
25. Alfred H. Barr is the author of the phrase; see Henry-Russell Hitchcock, *Architecture, Nineteenth and Twentieth Centuries* (Baltimore, 1958), pp. 380, 454, note 1.
26. Philip Johnson, "Whence & Whither: The Processional Element in Architecture," *Perspecta*, 9/10 (1965), p. 168.

27. *Ibid.*, pp. 171–172.
28. *Ibid.*, pp. 169–170.
29. Donlyn Lyndon, "Philology of American Architecture," *Casabella*, CCXXCI (November 1963), viii.
30. Robert Venturi, "The Campidoglio: A Case Study," *Architectural Review*, CXIII, No. 677 (May 1953), 333.
31. Robert Venturi, "A Bill-Ding-Board Involving Movies, Relics and Space," *Architectural Forum*, CXXVIII, No. 3 (April 1968), 75.
32. Donlyn Lyndon, "Philology of American Architecture," p. viii.
33. Robert Venturi, *Complexity and Contradiction in Architecture*, pp. 128, 133.
34. Robert Venturi, "A Bill-Ding-Board Involving Movies, Relics and Space," p. 76.
35. Charles W. Moore, "Plug It in, Rameses, and See if It Lights Up, Because We Aren't Going to Keep It Unless It Works," *Perspecta*, 11 (1967), pp. 40–41.
36. Robert Venturi, *Complexity and Contradiction in Architecture*, pp. 124–128. See also *Zodiac*, XVII (1967), 142–147.
37. Romaldo Giurgola, "Reflections on Buildings and the City: The Realism of the Partial Vision," *Perspecta*, 9/10 (1965), p. 108.
38. *Ibid.*, p. 112.
39. Romaldo Giurgola and Ehrmann Mitchell, "Young American Architects: Romaldo Giurgola & Mitchell" . . . Selection of Writings and Architectural Works," *Zodiac* XVII (1967), 132.
40. Willis N. Mills quoted in "A.I.A. Headquarters: Headquarters for Architecture?," *Progressive Architecture*, XLVII, No. 12 (December 1967), 140.
41. Donlyn Lyndon, "Sea Ranch: The Process of Design," in John Donat, ed., *World Architecture II* (New York, 1965), p. 31.
42. *Ibid.*, p. 33.
43. *Ibid.*
44. *Ibid.*
45. Barbara Stauffacher quoted in "Bathhouse Graphics," *Progressive Architecture*, XLVII, No. 3 (March 1967), 157–161.
46. Charles W. Moore quoted in "Implications of Giants," *Progressive Architecture*, XLVIII, No. 5 (May 1967), 159.
47. Charles W. Moore, "The Project at New Zion," *Eye: Magazine of the Yale Arts Association*, II (1968), 18–19.
48. *Ibid.*, p. 21.
49. Jane Jacobs, *The Death and Life of Great American Cities* (New York, 1961), p. 8.
50. *Ibid.*, p. 13.
51. Vincent J. Scully, Jr., "The Threat and the Promise of Urban Development in New Haven," *Zodiac*, XVII (1967), 171–175.
52. Vincent J. Scully, Jr., letter to the editor, *Journal of the American Institute of Planners*, XXXIV, No. 2 (March 1968), 127.
53. For a more extensive discussion of this project see Delma Denneby, "Progress in Strategy: New York Turns to 'Invisible Renewal' to Save its West Side," *Architectural Forum*, CXXIII, No. 1 (July-August 1965), 72–75.
54. Percy Johnson-Marshall, "The Shapes of the Southwest," *Architectural Forum*, CXV, No. 1 (July-August 1966), 64.
55. See Peter M. Green and Ruth H. Cheney, "Urban Planning and Urban Revolt: A Case Study," *Progressive Architecture*, XLVIII, No. 1 (January 1968), 134–156.

56. Peter Millard quoted in Donlyn Lyndon, "Philology of American Architecture," p. x. See also, my article, "The Office of Earl P. Carlin," same issue, pp. 183–198.

57. Peter Millard quoted in Stern, *op. cit.*, p. 190.

58. Ada Louise Huxtable, "Model Cities Construction to Start Here by Fall," *New York Times* (April 19, 1968), p. 49.

59. Charles W. Moore, "Plug It In, Rameses, and See if It Lights Up...," p. 36.

60. *Ibid.*

61. Robert Venturi, *Complexity and Contradiction in Architecture*, p. 133.

62. Wolf Von Eckardt, *A Place to Live: The Crisis of the Cities* (New York, 1967), p. 25.

63. For a more extensive discussion of this project see my article, "Constitution Plaza After One Year," *Progressive Architecture*, XLVI, No. 12 (December 1965), 166–171.

64. Charles W. Moore, "You Have to Pay for the Public Life," *Perspecta*, 9/10 (1965), p. 97.

65. Lawrence Halprin, *New York, New York* (New York, March 1968), p. 1.

66. James Stirling, "Conversation with Students," *Perspecta*, 11 (1967), p. 92. See also, Lawrence Halprin's analysis of the open space implications of the 1961 zoning ordinance in his *New York, New York*, pp. 90–95.

67. For an account of this group's work see Walter McQuade, "Inside Government," *Architectural Forum*, CXXVIII, No. 2 (March 1968), 86 and "The Assistant D.A.'s," *Architectural Forum*, CXXVIII, No. 3 (April 1968), 96.

68. Lawrence Halprin, *New York, New York*, p. 1.

69. M. Paul Friedberg quoted in Mildred F. Schmertz, "Designing the Spaces in Between," *Architectural Record*, CXLIII, No. 3 (March 1968), 128.

70. Charles W. Moore, "You Have to Pay for the Public Life," p. 65.

71. Robert Venturi and Denise Scott Brown, "Final Presentation: Learning from Las Vegas or Form Analysis as Design Research (The Great Proletarian Cultural Locomotive)" (10 January 1969), Yale University School of Art and Architecture, no page.

SELECTIVE BIBLIOGRAPHY

Books

Appleyard, Donald et al. *The View from the Road*. Cambridge, Massachusetts: M.I.T. Press, 1963.

Blake, Peter. *God's Own Junkyard: The Planned Deterioration of America's Landscape*. New York: Holt, Rinehart & Winston, Inc., 1964.

Hall, Edward T. *The Hidden Dimension*. New York: Doubleday and Co., 1966.

————. *The Silent Language*. New York: Doubleday and Co., 1959.

Halprin, Lawrence. *Cities*. New York: Reinhold Publishing Corp., 1963.

————. *Freeways*. New York: Reinhold Publishing Corp., 1966.

————. "New York, New York: A Study of the quality, character, and meaning of open space in urban design." Prepared for the City of New York, March 1968.

Jacobs, Jane. *The Death and Life of Great American Cities*. New York: Random House, Inc., 1961.

Jacobus, John. *Philip Johnson*. New York: George Braziller, 1962.

————. *Twentieth-Century Architecture: The Middle Years 1940–1965*. New York: Frederick A. Praeger, Inc., 1966.

Johnson, Philip. *Architecture 1949–1965*. New York: Holt, Rinehart & Winston, Inc., 1966. With an Introduction by Henry-Russell Hitchcock.

Le Corbusier, *The Radiant City*. New York: Orion Press, 1967; French edition, 1933. Translated by Pamela Knight, Eleanor Levieux, and Derek Coltman.

Lynch, Kevin. *The Image of the City*. Cambridge, Massachusetts: M.I.T. Press, 1960.

Mayor's Task Force. *The Threatened City, A Report on the Design of the City of New York*. New York, 1967.

Meyerson, Martin et al. *The Face of the Metropolis: The Building Developments that are Reshaping Our Cities and Suburbs*. New York: Random House, Inc., 1963.

Nairn, Ian. *The American Landscape: A Critical View*. New York: Random House, Inc., 1965.

Norberg-Schulz, Christian. *Intentions in Architecture*. Cambridge, Massachusetts: M.I.T. Press, 1961.

Ruscha, Edward. *Some Los Angeles Apartments*. Los Angeles: George Wittenborn, 1965.

————. *The Sunset Strip*. Los Angeles: George Wittenborn, 1966.

————. *Twenty-Six Gasoline Stations*. Los Angeles: George Wittenborn, 1962.

Scully, Vincent J., Jr. *Louis I. Kahn*. New York: George Braziller, 1962.

————. *Modern Architecture*. New York: George Braziller, 1961. See also Mr. Scully's forthcoming book on American architecture and urbanism.

Temko, Allan. *Eero Saarinen*. New York: George Braziller, 1962.

Venturi, Robert. *Complexity and Contradiction in Architecture*. New York: The Museum of Modern Art, 1966.

Von Eckardt, Wolf. *A Place to Live: The Crisis of the Cities*. New York: Seymour Lawrence/Delacorte Press, 1967.

Wolfe, Tom. *Kandy-Kolored Tangerine-Flake Streamline Baby*. New York: Farrar, Straus & Giroux, Inc., 1965. See Chapter I on Las Vegas.

Periodicals

Architectural Forum, New York.

Architectural Record, New York.

Perspecta, The Yale Architectural Journal, New Haven.

Progressive Architecture, New York.

Bottero, Maria, ed. "U.S.A. Architecture," *Zodiac: A Review of Contemporary Architecture*, XVII, Milan, 1967.

Mazzochi, Gianni, ed. "Archittetura U.S.A.," *Casabella continuatá, revista internazionale di archittetura e di urbanistica*, CCXXCI, Milan, 1963.

INDEX

SOURCES OF ILLUSTRATIONS

All illustrations are reproduced with the permission of the architects.

1. C. Hadley Smith, Ithaca, New York.
2. George Pohl, Philadelphia, Pennsylvania.
3. Charles R. Schulze, New Haven, Connecticut.
4. John Ebstel, New York City.
5. From *Louis I. Kahn* by Vincent J. Scully, Jr.
6. George Pohl.
7. From the office of Louis I. Kahn, Philadelphia, Pennsylvania.
8. George Pohl.
9. From the office of Louis I. Kahn.
10. Copyright, National Design Institute, India; photograph, Dalwadi P.M.
11. John Ebstel.
12. George Pohl.
13. Harold Feinstein, New York City.
14. Marvin Rand, Los Angeles, California.
15. From the publicity department of C.B.S., New York City.
16–22. From the office of Kevin Roche, John Dinkeloo Associates, New York City.
23. Chalmer Alexander, Hamden, Connecticut.
24–25. © Ezra Stoller (ESTO), Mamaroneck, New York.
26. Joseph W. Molitor, Ossining, New York.
27. Eagle Photo, New York City.
28. Joseph W. Molitor.
29. Bruce Cunningham-Werdnigg, Guilford, Connecticut.
30. © Ezra Stoller (ESTO).
31. From the office of Paul Rudolph, New York City.
32. Reprinted from *Architectural Record*, June, 1968, copyright © 1968 by McGraw-Hill, Inc., with all rights reserved.
33–34. © Ezra Stoller (ESTO).
35. From the office of Davis, Brody and Associates, New York City.
36. From the office of Paul Rudolph.
37. From the office of Philip Johnson, New York City.
38. © Maris (ESTO).
39–40. © Ezra Stoller (ESTO).
41. From the office of Philip Johnson.
42–43. © Ezra Stoller (ESTO).
44. Alex Georges, New City, New York.
45. Robert Perron, New Haven, Connecticut.
46. Louis Checkman, Jersey City, New Jersey.
47. From the office of Venturi and Rauch, Philadelphia, Pennsylvania.
48. Rollin R. La France, Philadelphia, Pennsylvania.
49. From the office of Venturi and Rauch.
50. George Pohl.
51. Robert Venturi, Philadelphia, Pennsylvania.
52–54. ©From the office of Venturi and Rauch.
55. George Pohl.
56. Robert Talboys of Clark & Rapuano, Inc., New York City.

57. Robert Venturi.
58. From the office of Venturi and Rauch.
59. George Alikakos, Philadelphia, Pennsylvania.
60. Rollin R. La France.
61. George Alikakos.
62–63. Rollin R. La France.
64. Romaldo Giurgola, New York City.
65. Rollin R. La France.
66–67. From the office of Mitchell/Giurgola, Philadelphia, Pennsylvania.
68. Romaldo Giurgola.
69. Randolph Langenbach, Boston, Massachusetts.
70. Rollin R. La France.
71. William Watkins, Philadelphia, Pennsylvania.
72. From the office of MLTW/Moore Turnbull, New Haven, Connecticut.
73–78. Morley Baer, Berkeley, California.
79. From the office of MLTW/Moore Turnbull.
80–81. John T. Hill, New York City.
82. From *Interiors*, December, 1968.
83. Mark Ellis, New Haven, Connecticut.
84. Aero Service Corporation, Litton Industries, Philadelphia, Pennsylvania.
85. © Ezra Stoller (ESTO).
86. From the office of I.M. Pei & Partners, New York City.
87. George Cserna, New York City.
88. J. Alexander, Wheaton, Maryland.
89. Jorgen Graugaard, Washington, D.C.
90. © Ezra Stoller (ESTO).
91. Jorgen Graugaard.
92–93. David Hirsch, Brooklyn, New York.
94. Bruce Cunningham-Werdnigg.
95. From the Office of Planning, Design and Research, Housing & Development Administration, New York City.
96. Hutchins Photography, Inc., Belmont, Massachusetts.
97. Ernest Braun, San Anselmo, California.
98. Joshua Freiwald, Berkeley, California.
99. Phokion Karas, Melrose, Massachusetts.
100. David Hirsch.
101–102. From the office of Davis, Brody and Associates.
103. Thomas Airviews, Bayside, New York.
104. From the publicity office of General Motors, New York City.
105. From "New York, New York" by Lawrence Halprin.
106. William F. Pedersen Architect and Associates, New York City.
107. Mark de Nalovy-Rozvadovski, New York City.
108. David Hirsch.
109. Charles Forberg, New York City.
110. From the office of I.M. Pei & Partners; Mark de Nalovy-Rozvadovski.
111. Balthazar Korab.
112. From the office of John M. Johansen, New Canaan, Connecticut.
113. From the office of Hardy, Holzman, Pfeiffer Associates, New York City.
114–115. From the office of Conklin & Rossant, New York City.
116. From the Rouse Company, Baltimore, Maryland.
117–118. From the office of Daniel, Mann, Johnson and Mendenhall, Los Angeles, California.
119. From the office of Paul Rudolph.